P9-BZR-577

Brighter by the Day

Brighter by the Day

Waking Up to
New Hopes and Dreams

ROBIN ROBERTS

WITH MICHELLE BURFORD

GRAND CENTRAL PUBLISHING

NEW YORK BOSTON

Grand Central Publishing
Hachette Book Group
1290 Avenue of the Americas, New York, NY 10104
grandcentralpublishing.com
twitter.com/grandcentralpub

First Edition: March 2022

Grand Central Publishing is a division of Hachette Book Group, Inc. The Grand Central Publishing name and logo is a trademark of Hachette Book Group, Inc.

Library of Congress Control Number: 2021949989

ISBNs: 9781538754610 (hardcover), 9781538710166 (large print), 9781538754627 (ebook), 9781538724330 (signed edition), 9781538724323 (B&N signed edition)

Printed in Canada

FRI

10 9 8 7 6 5 4 3 2 1

*To my glam fam, Elena, Petula, DiAndre, Jade,
and Nicole. You, along with my social media tribe,
make life brighter by the day.*

Contents

PART TWO

Positive On Purpose

PART THREE
Stronger Than You Know

Introduction

Dawn of a New Day

Even the darkest night will end and
the sun will rise.

—*From the movie* Les Misérables

I have my tribe to thank for *Brighter by the Day*. For seven months during the pandemic shutdown, I broadcast *Good Morning America* from a makeshift studio in my basement. Like a lot of folks, and maybe like you, I found myself craving connection. So each morning on social media, I read a short inspirational passage from a devotional and finished with a prayer. My tribe chimed in. "Wow, so it isn't just me feeling this way," many wrote in the comments section. Or: "This just speaks to me. How'd you know what was on my mind?" I didn't, but the Universe did. And truth is, I needed those pick-me-ups as much as those who heard them. Whether the topic was grace or contentment, compassion or resilience, I loved the reassurance that, in spite of the circumstances, brighter times were ahead.

Those social media posts started in my kitchen, with my longtime girlfriend, Amber, working the camera and our dog, Lil' Man Lukas, barking his amens. When I eventually returned to the studio, my tribe spoke up again. "Please don't stop the morning messages!" some wrote. So I began posting from my dressing room, often including my glam fam, the crew that works its magic to get me ready for the show. The boards lit up. "Where can I *read* your messages?" many asked. They'd come to rely on the a.m. boosts as much as I had and wanted them in written form. That is what inspired this book.

"My future starts when I wake up every morning,"[1] jazz great Miles Davis has been quoted as saying. That's how I feel when my lids slide open—not on all days, but most. By nature, I look for the good in things, yet I'm no Pollyanna. I'm not walking around handing out lollipops, singing "If You're Happy and You Know It." I recognize that life can be difficult, that we all go through times when we feel defeated.

Yet here's what I believe: Optimism is a muscle that grows stronger with use. Think about it. If you're an athlete who wants to improve your performance, you train. You do your planks and push-ups. Back when I played basketball, I'd get in the gym and shoot a hundred baskets. It's not by chance that we get better, faster, more fit. It happens because we do the work. We condition ourselves. The same is true with optimism. Embracing the bright side is a choice. One setback and situation at a time, we intentionally shift our viewpoint. Then when life throws us obstacles—and it will—optimism is our default. It's a habit we've formed over years.

Now, I can hear some of you saying, "Robin, this'll never work for me. I'm a pessimist." A handful of folks around me feel exactly that way. Believe me, I'm not here to tell you how to act, nor am I up on some holier-than-thou perch. I don't have all the answers, or even most of them, but hear me out. Not everyone naturally sees silver linings, but we can challenge ourselves to spot them. Many don't tend toward a sunny-side-up perspective, yet we can each use a dose of strength and hope. And that is, in a nutshell, how I define *optimism*—as hope. It's believing that no matter how high the hurdle, we'll find a way over it. It's trusting our own tenacity in the face of hardship. It's having the courage to dream and the passion to pursue our goals. And through it all, it's holding tight to the belief that no matter how bleak things get, nature's lights will come on tomorrow.

Brighter by the Day, I hope, will be your fresh start, a little light after a mighty tough season in our world. The last couple of years have been challenging for sure, a period unlike any we've ever experienced. We've made it through by lifting one another up, by realizing we're all in it together. What you'll find in these pages is more of that sharing, a conversation meant to remind us of what we already know—simple as that. As you read, imagine the two of us on a porch, swapping our best stories over kombucha, no sanctimony allowed.

I've organized the book into three parts, starting with "The Joy Mindset." In other words, how do you create a happy headspace? Stay with me. In "Positive On Purpose," we move our take on optimism—faith, bravery, fortitude, and boundless confidence—from principle to practice. And last,

"Stronger Than You Know" is both a nod to our capacity—we're far more powerful than we may realize—and a way to make optimism a long-term lifestyle.

That said, this framework is just a guide. Skip around if you'd like. Flip to the chapters you think will resonate, and take what works, leave what doesn't. I see this as a volume you might pick up in the mornings, or before you rest your head on your pillow at night. Or maybe you'll page through it when you're looking for a lift, when you need a word of encouragement. My only prayer is that after you close it, you feel more connected and less alone. That's what I believe we all want.

When it comes to recharging my own batteries, Key West is my happy place. Just thinking about my safe haven is enough to lower my shoulders and lift my mood. When Amber and I arrive there for a weekend, we do a ceremonial drive down Duval Street, the town's main drag, and then we stop at a gas station for Dion's fried chicken before heading to the house. There's no agenda beyond that.

We settle in, read, or sit out back by the pool, and mostly do nothing (except plan which of our favorite restaurants in town we'll go to next). The following morning, we're up early for the highlight of our stay, the island's spectacular sunrise. It never disappoints.

Word has gotten around about the magical daybreaks there. A group of locals who call themselves the Sunrisers gather daily on the pier to witness the splendor. A half hour before dawn, we hop on our rickety bikes, load Lil' Man Lukas in a front basket, and screech over to our favorite Cuban coffee spot. Moments later, we're out on the landing, chatting with neighbors as our dogs greet. But once those rays peek over the horizon, a hush descends. In stillness, we gaze out at the skyline, marveling at the miracle before us, soaking in the moment. My heart fills with gratitude for the chance to begin again.

Of the many dawns I've experienced on Key West, no two have ever been the same. On cloudy mornings, the golden rays streak through and paint the sky gold. Other times, the heavens are clear blue, reflecting the waters below. And always, there's that wondrous moment when light pushes away all darkness, when all remnants of night are dispelled. As I leave the pier, in awe once again of God's handiwork, I exhale and think, *I wonder how life will surprise me today.* That's not only my favorite line of lyrics from a song I once wrote with India.Arie. It's also how I approach each fresh round of sun. *What will be different this time? What will I learn? In what new ways will I be stretched?* However my day or yours unfolds, the gift is just having another. Let's cherish it.

Brighter by the Day

PART ONE

The Joy Mindset

Joy is the holy fire that keeps our purpose warm and our intelligence aglow.

—*Helen Keller,* Out of the Dark

Chapter 1

Happiness vs. Joy

Joy does not simply happen to us. We have to choose joy, and keep choosing it every day.

—Henri J. M. Nouwen

Happiness and joy are kinfolk for sure, yet there's a fair amount of daylight between the two. Happiness arises because of our circumstances. Joy sustains us in spite of them. Happiness is fleeting, a high note that slowly fades. Joy is the space between the notes, the flow that holds the music together. Happiness is a pursuit. Joy is a choice. And when it comes to shifting our mindset, that's where it all starts—with choice.

I thought of this while playing *Angry Birds*, my go-to way to chill. (And a shout-out to my friend Sam Champion, the beloved weather anchor, for introducing me, many moons ago, to the ultimate in escapism.) Amber recently chuckled when, after I'd delayed our dinner plans for "just one more round" of the game—did I mention it's addictive?—I found myself stuck at the same level. Three days and a whole lot of fuming later, I finally switched up my strategy, and within minutes, I'd won and moved up a rung.

That's when it struck me: *Angry Birds*, silly as it may sound, is a powerful lesson in making progress. Why do we keep doing the same things and expecting a different result? Psychologists call that insanity. I call it a reminder that we make no headway until we do.

I'll let you in on a secret: If your goal is to move toward a sunnier outlook—and I'm proud of you for even considering that act of self-love—you have to want it. Period. That goes for me as much it does for any of us. We can talk about optimism till the cows come home. We can pray, hope, and wish all year long. But unless we're ready to pivot—and then recommit to our new intention every day—it won't happen.

I once made this point during a speech, one my mom was there to hear. She must've thought I sounded full of myself, like I was implying that I've become who I am on my own, because during the ride home, she read me the riot act. "Think of all the people who've contributed to you," she said—and she was 100 percent right. Maybe I could've been clearer at the podium that evening, but here's what I was trying to say: Yes, I acknowledge that the tribe I was born into and the people I love have shaped my perspective in countless ways. I've had encouragement. I've had resources. I've had Good Samaritans and guiding lights along my route. And above all, I've had the stellar examples of my parents, Lawrence and Lucimarian Roberts, who made sure I believed anything was possible. Yet at the end of the day, I've had to *want* to see the good in the world, in others, and even in the most excruciating experiences. Those around me may have desired that for me, but only I could choose it. That's true for all of us.

I'm not on a soapbox, friend, but I am here with a gift. I'd like to pass on to you the gem my parents once gave me: You already have everything you need to forge a new path for yourself. I know you're fierce, because it takes chutzpah to consider a new course. And I'm betting that you've got hope that tomorrow can be better, 'cause otherwise, you probably wouldn't have picked up this little tome. And if we're going to take this journey together, the first step toward a positive outlook is—wait for it—readiness. It begins with saying to yourself, *I'm really going to give this joy thing a shot.*

By joy, I don't mean some sugarcoated version of reality. This isn't about faking your way through the day, masking despondency with a smile. Life is filled with disappointments and detours, losses and letdowns. I've lived through some myself and also mourned with others enduring tremendous heartache. The kind of joy I'm referring to is steeped in truth. It doesn't bury the low moments; it sees and accepts them. It doesn't disregard grief; it recognizes grief's place and purpose. When sadness creeps in for me, I think, *Okay, you're here, and though I'd rather not deal with you today, you have my attention.*

I've learned to honor the dark times as much as I do the bright ones, knowing that both will pass. What remains is what I still work to cultivate: a belief that, even as I navigate the peaks and valleys,

God cradles me in His palm. I will be okay even if the situation isn't. That's an assurance I rest in. That's a confidence I carry with me. And that is, as I see it, Joy, with a capital *J*.

My mother, who was full of mommy-isms I've loved sharing over the years, had her own phrase for a joy that acknowledges sadness. She called it "happy sorrow." In 2004, when my beloved father passed, our family lost its rock—and my mother lost her husband of more than fifty-five years. I'll always be grateful that some of my *GMA* colleagues, among them Diane Sawyer, Charlie Gibson, and Tony Perkins, made the trip to Mississippi to attend my father's homegoing service, held at the Triangle Chapel on Keesler Air Force Base. It was such a moving tribute to my dad's life and heroism. Afterward, with palpable sadness in the air, my mom and the rest of us filed out behind the casket as the choir sang the old gospel song "When We All Get to Heaven." What happened next still makes me smile.

Mom faced the choir, thrust her arms high in the air, and began directing. "No, no!" her voice rang out as I looked at her sideways. "More upbeat!" And just like that, the singers quickened their tempo, turning a somber refrain into one of jubilation.

Later, Mom told us why she'd done that. "Yes, your father is gone, and we hurt," she said. "But think of the joy he brought us. Think of all our wonderful memories of him. You can have sad sorrow or happy sorrow"—and she chose the latter. She did so not just on that day, but over and over throughout her years.

That idea has stayed with me. I even have a little placard that says HAPPY SORROW. Every time I glance at it, I chuckle at the thought of Mom directing that choir, and I also remember her wisdom. In our times now, none of us are walking around with a plastic grin, and we shouldn't be. No one's pretending all is well in a world gone topsy-turvy. There's uncertainty. There's vulnerability. There's sadness at times. And yet even when sorrow pays us a visit, it can take a seat alongside joy. The two can coexist.

In fact, joy and sorrow are interconnected. We can appreciate one only because we've experienced the other. When I think of my parents, both of whom have now gone home, I still well up. The loss pains me. But I choose not to dwell in that place, but rather to relish the good. I honor their legacies and give thanks for the many decades I had with them. Tears of joy are exactly that—grief and rejoicing in unison.

While I'm constantly striving for uppercase Joy, I also embrace its lowercase cousin. Happiness—the sheer bliss of, say, accomplishing a goal, or even just the tiniest of thrills—can bring us much-needed levity and laughter. We need to play, to lighten up and have some fun. Just seeing a colorful paper beach umbrella in a cold beverage makes me smile. That's such a small delight, but it instantly lifts my mood.

Music is another source of happiness. I grew up with my mother at the piano, with all of us gathered around singing. I still love it when my sister Dorothy visits and takes to the ivories the way Momma did, belting our mother's favorite hymn, "Blessed Assurance." And to this day, when I hear a favorite tune, it transports me. "Ain't No Mountain High Enough" was my theme song during cancer treatment—and, boy, did its lyrics get me through. When "September" by Earth, Wind & Fire comes on the radio, I've been known to break out dancing. I enjoy contemporary artists—Beyoncé, Adele, Taylor Swift, John Legend, the list goes on—but nothing gets my foot tapping like some old-school Motown and R&B. And Stevie Wonder? Any song by the musical master snaps me right out of a funk.

Our daily pleasures, however momentary, are cause for celebration. When happy feelings rise and recede—when our circumstances waver—joy is what anchors the soul.

Chapter 2

Make Your "One Day" Your Day One

You can't be that kid standing at the top of the waterslide, overthinking it. You have to go down the chute.

—*Tina Fey in* Bossypants

Ever find yourself saying, "One day I'll do this or that," only to put off your goal for weeks or months? You've got company. I've definitely had my share of false starts, my woulda-coulda-shouldas, my resolutions that went the way of the Walkman. That's real. But if being flat on my back taught me anything, it's this: Time is indeed precious, and cancer has a way of loudening the tocks. We're graced with a limited number of trips around the sun, and I've grown more and more determined to make each one count. So how about we flip the script together? Instead of saying, "I'll be more optimistic one day," let's make today our day one. Right here, right now, let's begin.

I get it. For some of you, focusing on your emotional health feels, well, selfish. I've heard from folks who are grappling with guilt, especially during these last couple of years, when we've had to step up in new ways for loved ones. Though the worst of our quake seems behind us—let us pray—the aftershocks continue. Families are grieving loss. Many weren't even able to say goodbye to their relatives and friends during their final moments, a heartbreak upon a heartbreak. Empty nesters have had their rhythms disrupted, with grown children who've moved home and maybe still haven't left.

In the beginning, many were excited to have family close again. But as weeks turned into months, often in tight quarters, all that together time brought inevitable bristling. And then there was the deep sense of disconnection during the shutdown. While some celebrated their newfound "me time," others, like some single people, felt profoundly isolated.

Our anxieties have lingered. I'm now getting in to see my doctors again, after lying low through much of the pandemic. One doctor mentioned that her patients have been clinging to her lab coat, pouring out their concerns in her office. "There's a real mental health crisis," she told me. When she has encouraged her patients to seek therapy, many have shrugged it off. "Oh, I'm fine," she has heard over and over.

She reminds them of what I'll share with you: It's okay not to be okay. Maybe you're emotionally drained, depleted by a long series of social reckonings and the conversations that go with them. Me too. In order to get help, we have to recognize that we need it.

In case you missed the memo, optimism runs through my veins. I come from a long line of idealists, strivers whose aspirations often eclipsed their means. In the 1930s, when Blacks were seen as second-class citizens in this country, my father had the audacity to dream of flying a plane. He'd disappear into the basement, take a sawed-off broom handle, and imagine it was his throttle. Many outside his family told him he was ridiculous: No way could a colored boy grow up to be a pilot. Daddy, however, was reared on the three *D*'s: discipline, determination, and da Lord. Powered by those principles, he pursued his goal, eventually serving in the United States Air Force as a colonel and becoming a distinguished Tuskegee Airman. And my mother—the first in her family to attend college (Howard University) and the first Black person to chair the Mississippi State Board of Education, just two of her many trailblazing accomplishments—was a ray of light and a pillar of faith. When I'm speaking to a group about my upbringing, about the inheritance I'm so thankful for, I can always tell when someone's eyes glaze over. *Good for you, Robin,* I can almost hear some thinking. *I'm glad you had great parents, but I didn't. This optimism stuff won't work for me.*

A woman I met actually voiced that viewpoint, and I offered her the answer I'll share with you: It has to start somewhere.

I'm the proud descendant of can-do visionaries, and someone down the line had to choose hope, choose faith, choose positivity. Wouldn't it be wonderful if, generations from now, your tribe could look back and say optimism began with you? Wouldn't it be an honor to launch that tradition, to leave such a light-filled legacy? A mighty oak grows from a tiny acorn. You could serve as your family's seed.

I love tennis legend Arthur Ashe's take on treading new ground: "Start where you are. Use what you have. Do what you can."[1] That thinking is what made him a sports icon, the only Black man to win Wimbledon and the US and Australian Opens—a champion.

In 2012, I decided to move a "one day" goal into the day-one column. That year, for me, was filled with transitions, some of them thrilling, others wrenching. I'd been diagnosed with MDS, a rare and deadly blood disease, and I received a lifesaving bone marrow transplant from my sister Sally-Ann. The words *thank you* don't quite cover it. Our sweet mother fell ill that same year and passed in the summer. *Oof.* Around that time, *GMA* reached a major milestone, becoming the number one morning show, at last breaking the *Today Show*'s sixteen-year run at the top. (And it was on that same momentous day, when Sam Champion and I danced the limbo on the *GMA* rooftop, that I'd learned of my MDS.)

Amid that whirlwind, I was yearning for a reset, a way to calm my nerves. To be honest, I wasn't sure meditation, or at least my notion of it then, would be right for me. The idea of "clearing my mind"—one sometimes racing with frets and Post-it notes to myself, travel plans and appointments—seemed unlikely. Enter my co-anchor George Stephanopoulos.

My job, like many, can be stressful. Not that I'm complaining, because as my friend tennis legend Billie Jean King is known for saying, "Pressure is a privilege"[2]—and she's certainly had some intense moments in her celebrated career. At *GMA*, however, privilege rarely gets a nap. My colleagues and I are always on the clock, rushing out the door to cover breaking news. Many stories are heartrending; others, frustrating.

On one morning, I felt like my head was going to explode after reporting something that was quite upsetting. I turned to George, thinking he'd be having the same reaction. But no . . . he was peace like a river. After the show I asked him for his secret. He told me about Transcendental Meditation (TM), a practice centered on *quieting* the mind, not clearing it. *All right, I'm listening,* I thought.

George connected me with his instructor, Bob Roth, who is, in a word, amazing. He's also patient, and he clearly explained the practice and its benefits. "Think of the mind as an ocean," he told me. "At the surface, it's often choppy. Waves are crashing. It's tumultuous at times. But miles below that turmoil, way down in the deep, the water is still. There's serenity. TM teaches us to access that stillness"—which, scientists have discovered, both slows the heart rate and invigorates the brain.[3]

Thoughts are not our enemy, Bob emphasized; they're part of being alive. You just close your eyes, allow your mind to roam, and when you start wondering what you'll have for breakfast—because if you're anything like me, you will—you gently push that thought to the side. How? By repeating your chosen mantra, a short word you keep private.

My first meditation with Bob was magical. I felt revived and empowered afterward. I immediately began the practice on my own, once or twice daily for twenty minutes.

My "day one" got underway well before sunup, as most of my mornings do. My alarm goes off at three fifteen, and I meditate between three thirty and four. After watching a few minutes of the overnight news, I'm in the shower by four thirty. On my way out the door, I say the Unity Prayer for Protection, the one my momma taught me when I first moved away from home: "The light of God surrounds me, the love of God enfolds me, the power of God protects me, the presence of God watches over me. Wherever I am, God is."[4] Then I meet my driver, Dario, downstairs and we listen to gospel music during the fifteen-minute drive to the studio. My talented glam fam, Elena (makeup artist), Petula (hairstylist), and DiAndre (clothing stylist), get me dressed and ready, putting Humpty Dumpty back together again.

At six thirty, I'm on set and preparing for the show, which is like being shot out of a cannon. We're on the air at 7:00 on the dot, not 6:59 or 7:01. At nine, we wrap up and start prepping for the next day. By early afternoon, my shades are lowering.

During my initial years on the show, before I'd found my groove, anyone who met me late in the day must've thought I was an idiot, because I could barely form a sentence by then. That's why, a couple of years ago, I changed my schedule. I now get up at four and do my first meditation right after the show. The second, if it happens, is before dinner. I try to be in bed no later than nine, to get at least six hours of rest. If I don't, then I'm running on fumes—and, trust me, that ain't pretty.

TM has turned out to be my stabilizing force. At the start of a session, I close my eyes and draw in a deep breath. *What do I smell? What do I hear? What am I feeling?* Recognizing these sensations as I settle in allows me to let them go later during the session.

I love TM because it's so forgiving. There's no right or wrong way to do it. I don't have to sit cross-legged. If I have an itch, I scratch. If I want to cough, I cough. Any and all experiences are okay.

Bob taught me that in those early months, when I returned to him for refresher courses. After that rapturous first session, I'd expected to experience the same the next morning. It didn't happen. Later when I saw Bob, I explained that my meditation didn't feel as deep or rewarding. What he said has stayed with me. "Sometimes you're in the shallow end of the pool," he said, "and sometimes you're in the deep end. Either way, you still get wet."

On those days when I'm down at the ten-foot end, I can feel the depth. My shoulders lower. I see brilliant colors in my mind. My ears start to pop, like they do when I'm on board a plane that ascends above the clouds. Some people say their stomach gurgles, but for me, it's the ear popping. I get excited when that happens. At other times, when I'm wading in the shallow end of the pool, my thoughts bounce all over the place: *What will I have for lunch? Did I ask the right questions in that last interview? What's on my schedule for the rest of the day?*

Whether I go deep or stay shallow, there's H_2O involved. I still feel the benefits of slowing down, breathing, and being present in the moment. For instance, an annoyance that I'd rate a two—like someone cutting me off in traffic—stays a two, rather than exploding into a ten. So while I may not have initially felt like a shallow meditation did me any good, Bob's wisdom now rings true: All wading is worthwhile.

I love it when my ears are popping and I'm seeing colors and I come out of the session thinking, *Score! Woo-hoo!* But that's not a feeling I chase every day. If it comes, it's a bonus. No two sessions are the same, nor should they be. Whatever happens is what should be happening. It's the one time (or two times!) in my day when I feel zero pressure to perform.

The secret to TM is to have no expectations. Let me say that again, only slower: There. Are. No. Expectations. *None.* I approach every session with what meditators call "beginner's mind," with no preconceived notions of what will happen. I welcome whatever shows up.

During the shutdown, Bob began offering recorded teleconference TM calls for thousands of people around the world. I dial in for the one at nine fifteen. DiAndre, Elena, and Petula stand guard outside my door. They know that this time is sacred. They've been my village for more than fifteen years, so they truly know me. As soon as I come off the set and go into my dressing room, they run interference. Anyone approaching my closed door has been met with a familiar refrain: "Please wait. Robin's doing her meditation."

I lower the lights, settle into a comfortable chair, and wrap myself in a colorful patchwork blanket. Once I'm on the line, I hear Bob's soothing voice, and the chaos of seven to nine falls away. "Release all expectations," Bob always says, "and I'll take care of the time." *Ahhh.*

Twenty minutes later, when he asks us to open our eyes, I usually have a big grin on my face. I sit there quietly, with the lights of Times Square flooding through the blinds. Bob shares a quote or a final thought. He then ends every meditation with a *bye* he drags out with a twang: "Byyyeee!" After, I'm like, *Let's do this, Robin.* I'm energized. I'm focused. I truly listen and connect. And most of all, I'm bursting with fresh ideas that I carry into the day.

Real talk: I've sometimes struggled with completing part two of TM. I'm a big fan of *King of Queens*, which happens to air at six, the same time as my evening meditation. *Come on, Robin,* I say to myself as I turn on the show, *you've seen this episode a million times!* Bob saved me from that battle. "You don't have to meditate at six," he said, chuckling. "Just dial in whatever time you get home"—which can fluctuate wildly. So since the session is recorded, I fit it in if I can. On the days it's not possible, I stop and take deep breaths. That truly calms and centers me. And when I meditate consistently, I notice a difference in myself.

For years, one of Bob's other students also struggled to get in the evening session. He so loved the benefits from the morning meditation that he didn't think he needed another. Still, he committed to it, and after a few months, he was like, "Wow, I can't believe I've been missing this." It was the same mix of serenity and vitality, only to the second power. The first meditation gears me up for the day. The second is how I wash off the day's cares, an evening bath for the soul. Both energize and relax me.

These past two years have been trying for all of us. The confinement and isolation of the pandemic have made many, myself included, reevaluate what matters most—to pause long enough for a breath and a close look. One thing I've discovered is the strength stillness brings. "Recharge your batteries, daughter," my father would often tell me when I was running ragged. Dad, as usual, was right. You hear that? It's the sound of the silence I soaked in, my respite from the noise of our world. My dear grandma Sally began her mornings with what she called her "quiet time." Her namesake, my sister Sally-Ann, does the same. My grandmother knew what I've since learned: Solitude reboots our minds and rejuvenates our spirits.

I'm in my tenth year of TM. And it began not with a big fireworks display or some grandiose plan, but with the teensiest of steps, simply with my thinking, *You know what? I'm going to try this.* My "day one" turned into a decade of exhales, so imagine where yours might lead. Particularly if optimism isn't your set point, ease into it. Reach for joy's low-hanging fruit. Greet a passerby on the street, just because. Look a friend or coworker in the eye, and really engage. Interrupt a negative thought with a slightly more cheerful one. Bring to mind a person or pursuit you've always been grateful for. Brighter by the day—that's the road you're on. Now keep going.

Chapter 3

Change the Way You Think to Change the Way You Feel

If you hear a voice within you saying,
"You are not a painter," then by all means
paint . . . and that voice will be silenced.

—Vincent van Gogh

One Monday last spring, I woke up feeling good—on top of the world, in fact. Soon after I arrived in my *GMA* dressing room, I pulled out my gratitude journal and made a list. Every morning, I write down at least two or three things I'm grateful for. "Thankful for a relaxing weekend with Amber," I wrote. "And thankful for my positive attitude." Later, after my glam fam had worked its usual abracadabra, I delivered my morning message and prayer on social media—about how breakdowns often lead to breakthroughs, how a so-called failure can pave the way to success. Amen.

That was at six forty-five. Moments later, as I was walking to the set, my bliss tank sprang a leak. The week before, I'd been dealing with an annoying issue I thought was settled. It wasn't, which I realized when I received an email. My producer, Nicole, happened to be passing me as I let out a loud "Argh!"

"Are you okay?" she asked.

"I will be," I said, though not at all convincingly. Right then and there, I had to check myself.

I drew in a couple of deep breaths, and as I slowly released them, I remembered a video I'd seen. In the middle of the pandemic, Tyler Perry posted a recording of an adorable, cherub-faced boy singing his rendition of the Bob Marley anthem "Every Little Thing Gonna Be Alright." That salve of a song had gone viral, which isn't surprising given the cuteness factor. When I'd first watched the video, it brought me a smile, and now, in that hallway, it gifted me with a turnaround. *Robin, what did you just write in your journal?* I thought. *You're not going to let this rob your joy. You're going to head downstairs, get on the air, and greet the nation.*

My job comes with a major perk. It's the best feeling in the world to say "Good morning, America" every single day. I mean that sincerely, and I never want that greeting to sound cookie-cutter. I think of it as saying, "Good morning, Amber," or "Good morning, Michael"—the warm, personal hello I'd offer a family member or friend standing right in front of me. For seventeen years and counting, it's been an honor to be invited into millions of homes for breakfast, to put a smile on people's faces. And aggravation aside, this time was no different.

I entered the studio, blew two kisses skyward to my mom and dad, as I always do, and took my seat at the anchor desk, truly believing that every little thing *was* gonna be alright. And no one was the wiser that, seconds earlier, I'd been ready to explode.

Were it not for my reset, courtesy of Tyler and years of practice at positivity, I might've gone out there wearing a scowl as I muttered my trademark hello. Instead, I reached for my mental remote and changed the channel. Folks can feel it when something's off with me, and I actually like that. I cannot fake the funk and don't want to. That's why I take a breath and center myself in the moment before I say, "Good morning, America." I want it to be genuine.

But when we declare ourselves optimists in training, that cues up pessimism's greatest hits: A chorus of negativity rings out. New fears take to the stage.

Doubt, that diva we thought we'd muted, belts out its solo refrain. This isn't coincidental. When we seek more of anything—courage, empathy, and, in this case, joy—our resolve will be tested. It's as if the Universe is saying, *You sure about that? Let me double-check.*

The challenge isn't meant to deflate us. Rather, it's there to deepen our determination. It's God's way of growing our capacity, of assigning us push-ups when we pray for, say, strength. It's how He gets us to turn up joy's volume when panic tries to interrupt. And right after I'd rehearsed my little joyous ditty, an email showed up to change my tune.

There's no Bubble Wrap around my mindset, no shield against annoyances. Anxieties creep in for me all the time. When life hands me lemons, I don't always make lemonade; sometimes I make a sour face. Just as they do for you, situations arise that spike my blood pressure and make my knees bob (which, by the way, is a family trait). And also like you, when my thoughts veer cynical, I choose whether to indulge or silence them.

When that note landed in my in-box, I'm thankful that I reached for the remote. I don't every time, because I have my weak moments, but the point is that I get to decide. I do so while gripping a principle I live by: We've got to change the way we think in order to change the way we feel. Writer Suzy Kassem put it another way: "Doubt kills more dreams than failure ever will."[1] Doubt, that sneaky rascal, is very agile—nimble enough to squeeze through the eye of a needle.

Among the bogeymen most capable of spooking us, uncertainty is high on the list. A few years back, as I was giving a commencement address, I peered out at the sea of graduates, wide-eyed with excitement at the yellow brick road before them yet apprehensive about what it might hold. I'd been exactly where they were, I told them. I remember sitting in the stadium at Southeastern Louisiana University, in my itchy cap and gown, with no job and no clue of what I'd do next. "You don't know what's coming," I told them, "and that can be scary. But you're going to figure it out, I promise. You've already got your own formula for success—that's why you're here. You went after what you wanted and found a way to get it. Trust yourself to do that again."

The same is true for you and me. When we set these lofty goals for ourselves, we often think, *Now how am I going to get there?* And yet we've previously scaled dozens of peaks, be they grassy hills or Everests. So why do we assume the mountains on the horizon are somehow insurmountable? Because we forget our own stamina. We dismiss our intelligence. We give negativity and naysayers too much airtime. We may not be as far along as we want, but we've managed to make it here. And the strategies we've used to move ourselves forward are exactly the ones we need up ahead. We're thrivers and don't even realize it.

So many brilliant people are afraid, and I so wish they knew we all are! Confidence isn't the absence of fear; it's the presence of mind to move through the trembling. "When you doubt your power," nineteenth-century novelist Honoré de Balzac is often quoted as saying, "you give power to your doubt."[2]

Your mind can be your most potent resource, as well as your greatest detriment. A single thought can send your spirits soaring or flatten them onto the sidewalk. *I'm not ready for this,* you may sometimes say to yourself when venturing into new territory. But while you may not have the skill, do you have the *will*? Could perseverance be your best play?

Or maybe you're battling the what-ifs. *What if I fall down? What if I'm not good enough? What if I get laughed clean out of the room?* When these questions surface for me—when doubt tries to give me lip—I've learned to counter with better queries: *What if I succeed? What if God's dream for me far surpasses my own? And so what if I stumble a thousand times, because who's really counting anyway?*

Sometimes we just have to leap and then grow our wings in midair. And if we indeed collapse onto the ground before us, a fall is still forward motion. We're going to take our spills. Our histories prove we'll somehow survive; otherwise, we wouldn't still be here.

After receiving that disturbing email, I quickly resolved the issue. And yet the lesson of that morning has lingered, become part of how I do life. I could've marinated in my anger all day. And don't think it wasn't tempting. That episode might've sent me spiraling, made me snippy with my coworkers and short on joy. I could've lashed out in resentment, but instead I took fast action and also took note—of a darling boy with an angel's voice who brought millions some musical comfort.

Chapter 4

Envision Your Victory

A vision is not just a picture of what could be; it is an appeal to our better selves, a call to become something more.

—Rosabeth Moss Kanter

I approach everything with a game plan. I'm an athlete at heart, a proud product of Title IX legislation, which leveled the playing field for this gangly girl in knee-high socks, as well as for myriad other strivers. The mind isn't simply a terrible thing to squander; it's also the sharpest arrow in our quiver. More than one basketball coach taught me that. The skills I learned in sports—focus, perseverance, teamwork, confidence, and, on the topic of this chapter, visualization—apply to many scenarios, including the goal of a joyful mindset. Triumph begins not out on the court, but in between our ears. Or, as author Richard Bach once wrote, "To bring anything into your life, imagine that it's already there."[1]

Turns out I have a decent imagination, or so I again realized in 2005. That entire period was turbulent. Suddenly and achingly, the fall before, I'd lost my dear father. It took me a while to find the happy alongside my sorrow. The *GMA* family, including our viewers, grieved with me, which is a big reason I emerged from that passageway whole.

Around then, I'd also just come out of an intense ten-year on-again, off-again romance, one with more bristling than calm. I was longing for a fresh chapter, a new and healthy relationship. For years, I'd been praying for the right person to come into my life; tagging along to dinner with friends as the third wheel gets old. So as I've done with all my desires, I began envisioning this one. I had a funny way of doing so.

One evening when friends and I were out at a favorite restaurant in Key West, a server we knew greeted us. "Will anyone else be joining you?" he asked, nodding toward the empty chair on my right.

"Yes," I said with a grin, "Tibba is coming."

Sensing that I was pulling his leg, he studied my face. "Who?" he said.

"Tibba," I repeated as my pals snickered. "That's how you pronounce TBA—to be announced."

That's right, people. I'd left a seat open for the

partner I believed was coming. The one I knew was out there somewhere. The one I fully expected to meet. My friends got in on the fun and even took it up a notch. "Will Tibba be here tonight?" they'd ask whenever we went out.

"Of course," I'd say. "She's on her way, and she'll be having the chicken."

The whole thing began as a joke, but I was only half kidding. That was my unusual way of graduating my self-talk to a kind of visualization.

My tribe had occasionally attempted to set me up. Let's just say that when it came to their picks, I might've chosen better blindfolded. So when my friend Bert mentioned he had someone in mind, I didn't cancel any plans. As fond as I am of my pal—hey, Bert!—his previous candidate wasn't my cup of tea.

This time, Bert said that his friend Alex knew a great woman, Amber, who then worked in fashion. The two of them thought she and I might be a great match. *I guess.* So for many months, Bert and Alex tried arranging a date, with plans for a four-way dinner. I hadn't seen a photo of Amber. And though she'd glimpsed me on *GMA* (in her office, they regularly watched the *Today Show*... ouch), she hadn't followed my career. She knew as little about me as I did about her.

First, I canceled. Next, Amber did. And then three weeks later, on the morning of our third effort, a friend mentioned to Amber that I wasn't on the air. "Maybe that means she won't be there tonight," she'd said hopefully. But on that evening, we both showed up. Our great dinner conversation spawned many others, in what was clearly a deep attraction. Seventeen years and countless heart-to-hearts later, sweet Amber and I are still rolling strong. By the way, the joke lived on: For months, my friends called her Tibba. She didn't show up on that first night I left open a seat, but sure enough, Amber eventually came along.

Amber and I met in summer 2005. Soon after, Hurricane Katrina ravaged the Gulf Coast and decimated my hometown of Pass Christian, a Mississippi treasure locals call the Pass. In May of that same year I'd become co-anchor of *GMA*, and I was delighted to share the desk with Diane Sawyer and Charlie Gibson. Eighteen months later, I was diagnosed with breast cancer.

"I know you didn't sign up for this," I told Amber then, but her devotion did not waver. She cared for me through chemo, when I had tubes coming out of every orifice in my body, two stray hairs left on my head, and a body that shrank from 150 pounds to 105; through a grueling stem cell transplant; through MDS, a potentially fatal blood disorder; and through the other bumps and heartaches that come with just breathing.

Key West is my happy place, and Amber is my joy personified. I'm the extrovert in the house (Amber's never encountered a spotlight she didn't shun), and yet we're both consummate homebodies. Few experiences bring me more pleasure than relaxing with Amber in our backyard, with no plans and no desire to make any.

Not that our relationship is all blue skies and cotton candy. People often say to us, "You two are 'couples goals' "—as in the hashtag equivalent of an ideal pair. If by that they mean a couple who has spent months in counseling and has made a real effort to reinforce our bond, then, yes, that is true. Like most couples, we've had our rough patches. Our first year together? North of amazing. But in the lead-up to our second anniversary, I began inwardly debating whether we'd go the distance.

My doubts, I now know, were connected with my own history. When I met Amber, I'd recently ended a long combustion of a relationship, one that so conditioned me for chaos that I unconsciously equated it with love. That is why my easy rapport with Amber felt emotionally unfamiliar. I had no script for romantic serenity, no blueprint for a drama-free union. So, harkening back to my old self, I told Amber I wanted to move on.

Fully aware of my old dynamic, she locked eyes with me and said, "If that's what you want, Robin, then knock yourself out."

Whoo! I'd been ready to hear, *Oh, please, you can't leave me,* but Amber had said just the opposite.

"I'm not going to be in a break-up, make-up kind of relationship with you," she then said.

Well, that sat me up straight. "No, no, no," I told her, "that's not what I meant." I so respected her firm stance. That's one of many reasons for our longevity.

Years later, I felt myself reverting to an old thought pattern: Maybe if I made Amber's life miserable enough, she'd break up with me. If she bailed, then I wouldn't be to blame for ending our long-standing partnership.

In my heart, I knew that wasn't the solution. A friend I confided in suggested couples counseling. I hesitated to bring it up with Amber—I wasn't sure she'd be open to it—until the evening when I knew that if I didn't clear my throat, things would be over between us.

We were walking home from dinner and I broke down crying, right there on a street corner on New York's Upper West Side. I explained that I wasn't happy with us and wanted to figure out why. "We need counseling," I said with a trembling voice. "I don't like who I'm becoming or some of the ways I'm treating you."

The fact that I was so emotional in public was an indication to Amber how dire the situation was. She immediately agreed.

Our therapist was incredible and beyond patient. In place of advice, she gave us tools, so we could find the answers ourselves. Our issue boiled down to communication—the manner and, at times, the lack thereof. When we did talk, we often spoke past one another. The counselor gave a suggestion that turned out to be extremely helpful. When Amber and I found ourselves in a heated discussion, with each of us intent on getting a point across—and with one or both of us feeling misunderstood—we'd gesture to halt the conversation, no questions asked. How? By tapping our own shoulders (in basketball, that's a signal for a twenty-second time-out). After regrouping, we'd usually return much better able to truly listen. We worked with the therapist for a year, and our growth became the glue that strengthened our connection.

The most important relationship of my life began with a steadfast conviction and a (mostly) blind date. Months before Amber and I went out, I trusted that love was imminent and certain. I'm fortunate that it was. It's not that one's belief guarantees a romance, or anything else for that matter. But hoping for the best—and then visualizing that hope—is like turning on your spiritual taxi light. You're signaling your intentions to the Universe, and it joins you in manifesting that desire. You're open, you're ready, and you're expecting good things.

That's how I approach every part of my life. Another of my mottoes: Dream big, focus small. I've always felt my focus on the finish line was a factor in my beating cancer—twice. The Big C was my opponent. The doctors were my coaches. The treatment was my game plan. The one-hundred-day mark after my stem cell transplant was the goal I stared down.

I'm in no way suggesting that those succumbing to illness have weak faith. I also believe God's in control of the number of breaths we get. When I meet someone who has suffered the loss of a loved one, I assure them that though the outcome wasn't what they'd hoped and prayed for, their loved one's fight was every bit as valiant and meaningful as anyone's.

And even if there's no discernible evidence of visualization's efficacy, there's proof that when we meditate, when we exhale, when we smile and laugh and hug, we lower our blood pressure and release endorphins. That's a compelling reason to stay on the positive path. And where might that path lead? TBA. Life will surely surprise us.

Chapter 5

Give Thanks for the Glass

Enjoy the little things, because one day
you may look back and realize
they were the big things.

—*Robert Brault*

The book *My Story, My Song* was Momma's love letter to the world, her warmth and wisdom memorialized. I'll always recall the night she was completing it. There I sat, near her in her family room, balancing my laptop on my knees, as I helped her with the acknowledgments. "Who would you like to thank?" I asked her. She pushed her glasses up on her nose, sat back in her recliner, and said, "Where do I begin?" Well, once she got started, she didn't stop. In addition to her poignant words for family, she thanked every doctor who'd ever taken her blood pressure, all the many church members she adored, and nearly a hundred friends and acquaintances. When I gently suggested she trim her list, she turned to me and smiled. "Oh, honey," she said, "you can't put a limit on gratitude."

Mom kept an aphorism in her pocket, ready to pull out when the Spirit prompted. "If ifs and ands were pots and pans, there'd be no need for scrubbing," I can hear her saying to my siblings and me. Or "When you strut, you stumble," which was what she pointed out to us to keep us from getting cocky. And then there was this saying, as much a warning as a truism: "A hard head makes a soft behind," meaning insolence could bring a whupping.

Of the many jewels my mother left our family, her reverence for thanksgiving is among our most prized. Gratitude, for Mom, was the holy grail. She lived it. She embodied it. She spoke often of the angels who'd lit her way, like her second-grade teacher, Wilma Schnegg-Merold, who supported her through college and even once organized a recital to raise the tuition Mom needed to stay at Howard, when money ran short during her junior year. And on the evening she was finishing her book, as she insisted on thank-you after thank-you, Mom's point was that we can't overdo it.

"When I started counting my blessings," Willie Nelson once said, "my whole life turned around."[1] Boy, can I relate, Sir Willie. During my dual showdowns with cancer, I brought my gratitude A game. I knew I had just two plays: I could allow the illness to destroy and define me, to permanently cripple my spirit. Or I could embrace the experience as a rebirth, as a butterfly struggling against the walls of its cocoon, and getting stronger as it does. Like the thousands who've inspired me on this road, I chose not only to survive but to thrive. I also reached for my leather journal.

Every morning, I cataloged my miracles, my godsends great and small. Like the afternoon God sent one of my angels, Diane Sawyer, into my chemo room with Popeyes chicken (she even remembered my fave: two pieces of white meat, spicy), in observance of my last chemo treatment. Or the glorious day, six months after I'd been quarantined while fighting MDS, that I returned to the *GMA* set, with frail body but warm heart. Or the many fun moments after my recovery, like when I'd spontaneously cut a two-step with Amber in our kitchen, or when a friend would crack me up till my side ached. Our bounty is as plentiful as it is healing; it shores up our bliss and renews our vision. Because when you're sitting in solitude for 174 days straight, you begin to view the world through a new lens. People often see the glass as half-empty or half-full. I simply see the glass.

Carlos Calloway can attest. Last year, I had the privilege of following him and five others in desperate need of organ donation, for the Discovery Plus series *Last Chance Transplant*. After Carlos, a Nashville husband and father, was diagnosed with stage 4 kidney disease, he spent nine to twelve hours a day on dialysis. A dozen of his loved ones stepped up to offer him a kidney, but heartbreakingly, none were a match. "It flashed through my mind, 'How much longer do I have with Carlos?' " said his wife, Juanita, with a tremble in her voice. They sent out an email blast to the parents at their children's school and prayed for a miracle.

Enter Adam Twining, a dad of three and husband to Christy, a former transplant nurse. When Adam read that a fellow parent at his daughter's school needed help, he texted the couple and offered his kidney.

"I was really overwhelmed that a complete stranger was willing to make this sacrifice," recalled Carlos, squelching tears.

Soon after the Calloways received that life-changing news, Carlos and Adam connected in person. It was the start of what Carlos calls a brotherhood for life: two fathers, one Black, the other white, with a bond transcending the social barriers we too often put up.

"The amazing thing about kidney donation is that you just need to be a human to donate to another human," Adam said. "It doesn't matter your race, religion, ethnicity... As long as we're medically compatible with the same blood type, it's a green light to go."

Added Carlos: "As my grandmother would say, we all bleed the same color, we're all part of the human race... I can see that Adam has the same mindset."

Adam underwent two months of testing and

discovered he was indeed a match. The fathers went into surgery as their nervous families stood by. Both men came through the procedure smoothly and awakened to the best news: Adam's kidney had immediately taken to its new home.

I still tear up when I think about Carlos's first question when he came out of anesthesia. "How's Adam?" he wanted to know.

In a triple-Kleenex conversation on FaceTime, the two men shared a beautiful connection. "I really want to thank you," said Carlos, trailing off into tears.

"You're my brother and my friend," Adam told him, "and I wouldn't have it any other way."

Carlos is just one of the courageous thrivers I marvel at. I'm also in awe of the scores of thrivers surrounding me, not just those who've defied cancer by God's grace, but the many who've withstood other scorching Saharas. Every year on my "rebirth day," the anniversary of my bone marrow transplant, viewers send me such touching stories. Some have turned the tragic into the hopeful; others have rebounded from homelessness and bankruptcy; and all have come through with their palms pressed together.

In 2018, I began nudging these overcomers into the limelight, with a digital series known as #Thriver-Thursday (ThriverThursday.com). My social media fam has gotten in on the gratitude action, with our weekly round of #ThankfulThursday. I end every post with an invitation: "Let us know what you're most thankful for." The message boards light up with all sorts of testimonials, from the outright comical to the tear-jerking. Long after I've gone on to other things, my followers will continue the conversational thread, throwing out encouragements like, "Hey, tribe, thinking of y'all...have a good day." I love that.

So what does all of this have to do with optimism? I'm glad you asked. Because where thankfulness flows, joy goes. Gratitude lifts your cheeks and lowers your temperature, all while bathing your brain in dopamine. The practice is both good medicine and good sense. And whether you express appreciation by hand (I still jot my thank-yous in my diary, at times while I'm relaxing in my rockin' red sitting room) or by voice (try channeling Stevie: "I just called... to say..."), there are innumerable upsides to the grateful way.

Just as there's no limit on thankfulness, there's no lid on its rate of return. "Gratitude unlocks the fullness of life," says author Melody Beattie. "It turns what we have into enough, and more. It turns denial into acceptance, chaos to order, confusion to clarity. It can turn a meal into a feast, a house into a home, a stranger into a friend."[2]

It can also turn a simple gathering into a party rivaling Mardi Gras. Back in 2005, I traveled to South Africa with former president Bill Clinton, to learn about his foundation's AIDS initiatives. While I enjoyed my interview with him, the trip's highlight came from an unexpected place. To get a better sense of that part of the world, one I'd never visited, I went with an interpreter into some impoverished areas, villages with no electricity. Along a dirt road, I spotted a group of women in colorful garb, dancing and singing and chanting in the front courtyard.

We approached. "Is it a holiday?" I asked through the translator. The response they gave still lights me up. "They are celebrating life," the interpreter told me. "That is all."

Wow. These women didn't even have running water, and here they were, with exuberance on their faces, with hands raised skyward for the privilege of breathing. We often label our days as good or bad, when just being alive is a boon. As I've been known to say of myself: Hot mess, still blessed—and above all, still here.

No need to save up our *gracias* for #Happy-FridayEve. God's favor shows up 24/7 in the littlest gestures. (Ever notice how a compliment brightens your mood? Let's pass on that uplift to others.) It also turns up in the kindness of loved ones. Amber overhead me saying that all I wanted for my fiftieth birthday was dinner and dancing with friends on the beach, and while a rare storm had a different idea, I was moved by her thoughtfulness to make my idea a reality.

We all have the desire to be seen and heard, to

know that we've contributed. William James put a beautiful spin on that notion: "The deepest principle in human nature is the craving to be appreciated."[3] So true. Why not satisfy that yearning for someone who least expects it? The gift is in the giving.

PART TWO

Positive On Purpose

We can't just hope for a brighter day,
we have to work for a brighter day.

—Dolly Parton

Chapter 6

Dream Big, Focus Small

The trouble with not having a goal is that
you can spend your life running up and down
the field and never score.

—Bill Copeland

Positivity comes with no cruise control. We can't just embrace joy once, sit back, and expect to run on automatic. We've got to keep on choosing a sunny perspective, shifting our mindset purposefully. On the bright side, you and I are learning to drive a stick shift. On the dazzling side, the best part of the journey is up ahead. Let's get in gear.

In these pages, *optimism* has had its aliases. I've called it *hope*—our belief, amid storm clouds, that a beach day is coming. I've named it *courage*, as in staring down life's frightening Goliaths. It also happens to be wide-eyed, a dreamer with grand ambitions and the discipline to achieve them. "A goal without a plan is just a wish," says a proverb I love. In my days as an athlete, my coaches echoed that point and anchored it with another. "A dream becomes a goal only when you write it down," I heard them say.

And a goal becomes a triumph one intentional move at a time.

I'm big on the little things. We come up with these giant resolutions that we'll get out of debt, run a marathon, start a business . . . fill in the blank. And yet months later, we're still in the starting block. Why? In part because we don't break our pursuits into specific, doable actions.

We also forget there's a wide canyon between a wish and a goal. A wish makes butt prints on the sofa. A goal laces up its sneakers. A wish flaps its gums all day long, while a goal maps out a clear strategy. Walt Disney, the fourth son of a farmer, sketched his first major animated character, Oswald the Lucky Rabbit, in 1927, before movies even had sound. Mr. Disney knew the secret. Imagine—yes. Pray—for sure. Dream, and keep on dreaming. But when you wish upon a star, also grab a pen and paper.

I've always logged my aspirations, even when I couldn't yet spell them. During my senior year of high school, I listed my career goals on a whiteboard that hung on my bedroom wall. In block letters, I wrote a title: *S-U-C-E-S-S*. I might've been one *C* short in 1979, but I was already on to something. By then I'd decided I was interested in broadcasting, just like my older sister Sally-Ann. So underneath my heading, I detailed my game plan, bullet point by bullet point. I'd start out in a small market, take my cuts while in the minors. From there I'd move to a medium-sized station, and then at last on to my dream job—as a reporter/anchor at ESPN. Each stage came with a timeline: *x* years here, *x* years there, until I sat in that *SportsCenter* anchor chair.

In hindsight, I chuckle at my nerve, passed on to me by two undeniable pioneers, also known as my parents. No Black woman had ever accomplished the feat I'd outlined. I hoped to do it by 1990.

What I lacked in work history I made up for in pluck. While still a university student, and long before internships were a thing, I showed up at a family-owned country music station, WFPR radio in Hammond, Louisiana. I asked the owner, "Big John" Chauvin, for a job as a sports director. The position didn't exist. So instead I started as assistant news director, soaking up as much experience as I could, and once even soaking my pants. (That's right: I was so rattled during my maiden live newscast that I peed on myself, and then I backed out of the room to hide the evidence.) Big John and his wife, Frances, known as the Pie Lady, and their large family, were revered and beloved in the community. They and Mary Pirosko, WFPR's news director, truly embraced me. They taught me what it means to be a mentor.

While working as assistant news director, I continued begging to host my own sports show. The Chauvins, tired of my hounding, relented on one condition: I'd have to deejay on weekends. *Count me in,* I said to myself. I (half) jokingly signed off my broadcasts with a line that proved my focus: "And this is Robin René Roberts for ESPN." I can still hear the teasing from my college basketball teammates.

Focusing small meant paying my dues, as well as keeping my eyes on the prize. That's why, when I graduated from Southeastern Louisiana University in

1983, I did something that even my family deemed foolish: I turned down a full-time news anchor position, paying $15,000 a year, and instead took a part-time sports job in Hattiesburg, Mississippi.

"News is more prestigious," said many who urged me to reconsider. But I stood firm in my reasons, all of them rooted in that whiteboard list. First, I thought of *news* as a four-letter word, and I wanted nothing to do with it. Also, the news position would've diverted me. The part-time gig, which paid a paltry $5.50 an hour for thirty hours a week with no benefits, was as a weekend sports anchor—a role that would point my toes toward ESPN. In that era, women were scarce in sports television, especially in front of the camera. I'd been struggling even to get an interview for a sports job, while offers in news abounded. So when WDAM-TV cracked open a door, it was, *Hattiesburg, here I come.*

That choice altered my course in exactly the direction I'd hoped. Yes, I was broke as a joke in my home state. My rent was $242, nearly all of my paycheck, and a drive-in movie was a splurge. But the experience became a stepping-stone to other goals, though I never viewed it as just a temporary stop... I learned so much from the respected veterans there. I next landed a job at WLOX-TV in Biloxi, on the coast, a slightly larger small market that gave me plenty of room to grow. *Check.*

That led me to Nashville's WSMV-TV, a well-regarded station not just in that region, but all over the country. (It had won prestigious Peabody Awards, and also, here's some trivia: Long before the talented Pat Sajak became host of *Wheel of Fortune*, he'd been a weatherman there.) With the nurturing guidance of news director Alan Griggs—Oh, how that man made me feel valued!—I sharpened my anchoring skills, as well as learned to hold my own on live television. I was honored to be named sportscaster of the year by a local paper, and giddy to be on track with my plan. Turning down that first news job had been my number one smartest choice. My number two best decision soon followed.

In 1987, ESPN came a-callin'—a full three years

earlier than I'd planned. Be still, my heart. A competing Nashville station had sent my tape to ESPN, hoping I'd get hired away and thus clear the path to the top spot in the ratings. My interview at the network turned out well, although the execs weren't quite clear on what my role would be if I decided to join the team. Meanwhile, during this same period, I was offered a position as a sports reporter at Atlanta's WAGA-TV, a top market, much larger than any I'd worked in.

I suddenly had a choice to make, one that seemed like a no-brainer to everyone in my ear. But much as I'd been salivating over ESPN, I knew I needed more experience. My heart told me that, and so did God. He often speaks to me through my inklings, and His message couldn't have been clearer: *Child, you ain't ready.* Was I over the moon to be considered? Abso-freaking-lutely. Still, I couldn't quiet that little voice, the one whispering, *Come on, girl, let's get real.* I was just a few years out of college and a long way from being seasoned.

As I saw it, I'd probably have just one chance at ESPN, and if I was going to take the shot, I wanted to be prepared. Then if it didn't work out, okay, but at least it wouldn't have been because I aimed prematurely. That, I could live with. What I couldn't handle was possibly being a blip—now you see me, now you don't. I wanted staying power. I wanted to go in strong and build from there. Many thought I was crazy to pass on a job I'd been eyeing for years, but the Lord had something else in mind. He gave me the confidence to board the midnight train to Georgia and embrace the opportunity at WAGA.

I'm glad I trusted both God and my gut, because the experience served as a footbridge. For the first time, I covered major pro sports teams: the Falcons, the Braves, the Hawks. I also became a radio personality at V-103, a top-rated urban contemporary station. I cohosted a show with "Mike Roberts in the morning, yeah!"—his tagline—and relished interviewing stars like Will Smith, Smokey Robinson, and Deion Sanders. I loved all things ATL—the city, my work, and, most of all, the people. And then, two years into that magic carpet ride, ESPN rang again. Oh, happy day!

My time in the Peach State had stretched me as a journalist, so on this go-round, I was ready. Still, unbelievably to most, and even to me, I initially hesitated. Atlanta felt like home, and relocating to Connecticut (the network is headquartered in Bristol) would mean missing the scores of relationships I'd invested in. My family would also be what felt like a world away. And then there was the issue of pay—as in less. I'd have to take a cut.

The deciding factor became the enthusiasm of John A. Walsh, then managing editor of *SportsCenter.* He seemed absolutely convinced that I'd blossom at ESPN, and his passion and strong vision spilled over onto me. Not only did he hire me as the network's first Black female anchor, but he also became a great mentor, advocate, and friend.

That was in 1990—right in line with my written goal, and apparently on point with God's master plan. At age twenty-nine, I was living my dream. You name it, I covered it, play by play, while wearing a huge grin and a mullet hairstyle: Wimbledon and the US Open; the Olympics (my first was the 1992 Games in Barcelona); the NBA Finals; the Super Bowl; on and on. I also contributed regularly to *NFL PrimeTime* and even had my own series, *In the SportsLight*.

Some folks called me an overnight success. I called myself the slow-but-steady tortoise, on the crawl-up for a decade. I'd learned so much in those early markets, a foundation I still stand on. At ESPN, I thrived for fifteen years before transitioning to the *GMA* anchor desk. What a head-spin. What a round of manna from heaven. Dream big, focus small.

I've been told no a lot during my career. Folks said I couldn't break into sportscasting. Couldn't advance to a larger TV market. Couldn't move to the national level. Every no supercharged my motivation, empowered me to push.

What is someone saying that you can't do? Get a promotion? Beat an addiction? Get married? Trade cantankerousness for warmth? Take your cue from this proverb: "Think of many things. Do one."

Getting ahead is about getting started. You can do that, can't you? Sure you can. When in doubt, take the next baby step. Then another. And another. Success, no matter how you spell it, begins with a half inch forward.

Chapter 7

When Fear Knocks, Let Faith Answer

The most difficult thing is the decision to act.
The rest is merely tenacity.

—*Amelia Earhart*

Turning the Tables with Robin Roberts grew out of a simple question: What would happen if I brought together a group of trailblazers over tea and intimate conversation? The result is the Disney Plus series—all Earl Grey and no wine, thanks to the query that led to it. The program launched in 2021. For the first episode, I gathered with three entertainment dynamos, Debbie Allen, Jenna Dewan, and Sofia Carson. Once we'd settled into our chat, Debbie, in keeping with the show's title, spun the lazy Susan around to me.

"What was your biggest interview that gave you a little stage fright?" she asked.

"Ooh, I'm gonna get real right here," I said, sitting back on the couch. "I can't believe I'm going to share this."

I almost didn't. For a half second I thought, *Is this the right format?* But before I knew it, I was opening up about a day when fear tapped on my door. Spoiler: Faith wasn't home.

It was May 2012. President Barack Obama's reelection campaign had recently gotten underway when then vice president Joe Biden signaled his endorsement of marriage equality—a stance Obama hadn't yet publicly taken. That week, the White House rang ABC News with a request: The president wanted to sit down for an interview with me. During our taped one-on-one, he'd likely voice his support for same-sex marriage. Clearly, it would be a watershed moment. It just happened to arise at a shaky one for me.

The world knew I'd come through cancer in 2007. What I hadn't yet revealed is that I'd been diagnosed with MDS, the blood disorder that prompted round two of my health battle. My oncologist had given me a soul-crushing prognosis: I had a life expectancy of one to two years. *Oof.* On the morning I heard that news, I was still reeling between bewilderment and numbness when the president's request came in.

I hesitated to do the interview not because of my health crisis, but because I was scared I'd be outed.

Mind you, I'd never been "in the closet," a phrase that irritates me. Society doesn't pressure heterosexual folks to "come out" and declare how and whom they love. Also, I wasn't hiding. "You're the most openly closeted person I've ever met," someone once said to me. Around town, I always introduced Amber as my girlfriend, and my colleagues and certainly my family had known for years that I'm gay. I still get chills when I recall what my mother, a devout Christian, once told me. "You are my child and a child of God, and He loves you because of who He is, and not because of anything you do or don't do," she said. Thank you, Momma. Still, I'd felt no desire up to that time to put my private business on loudspeaker. I feared, perhaps needlessly, that the interview would bring attention to my sexuality—so much so that I nearly declined the invitation of a president.

I'm grateful that good sense runs in my family,

and I quickly talked some truth to myself. *Robin René Roberts, are you kidding?* I thought. *This man is going to change countless lives, and you're afraid you're going to be* outed?

I have to laugh at myself when I look back on it because my dread had temporarily blinded me. This milestone had nothing to do with me personally. It was about justice for the scores of same-sex partners whose commitments, however solid, hadn't ever been legally recognized. It was an affirmation that love is love, a nod to the valiant servicepeople who've defended a nation that would finally view their unions as valid. It also underscored how swiftly public opinion had changed, with approximately half of Americans supporting marriage equality. And yet when the White House rang on that Monday, I got caught up in my stage fright.

A little self-talk goes a long way. Because on that Wednesday, sitting across from the commander in chief in the Cabinet Room, I leaned forward and asked what was on the minds of millions: Had the president changed his stance on marriage equality?

After explaining how his thinking had evolved, he answered in the affirmative: "I think same-sex couples should be able to get married," he said.[1] His statement, of course, made international headlines, as revelers and supporters welled up with happy tears. When I look back on the hundreds of interviews I've been honored to take part in, that one is among those I'm most thankful for. And it came *this close* to not happening.

When anxiety marches into the foyer, it seldom cowers. Occasionally, it raps softly and mumbles hello, but more often, it pounds. It rails as it beats its fist on the oak, furrowing our brows. And the issue becomes, as it did for me, whether fear or faith will respond. So the next time you glance through your door's peephole and spot panic on the porch, how will you steel yourself for the standoff? Look not in a guidebook but in the mirror, because your life is teacher of the year. Our experiences, and especially the agonizing ones, have a bounty of lessons to lend us.

But first, a brief programming note: All fear is not

created equal. Some doubts and frights are signaling that you're not ready, like the gut feeling that led me to turn down the team at ESPN when they initially approached me. Good call. Other alarm bells are telling us to sprint—when we sense danger on a desolate street corner or when we need to flee abuse. Heed the warning. The fears I'm learning to fend off are the irrational ones, like those insisting that I can't, despite evidence to the contrary, or those that are just downright crazy—as in the sort that might've robbed me of an exclusive with the leader of the free world. No one's suggesting that you plan a picnic in a lion's den. We're talking about smart leaps here, audacious acts that push us out of our comfort zones and toward fulfillment.

I can't remember a chapter in my life when I wasn't frightened for one reason or another. My earliest memory was the year my father retired from the military. I'm the youngest of four children, and what a gift to be Butch, Sally-Ann, and Dorothy's baby sista. I'm also a proud, bona fide military brat. I still recall answering our phone with, "Colonel

Roberts's quarters, Robin speaking!"—because *quarters* sounded more stately than plain ol' *residence*. I loved everything about our lifestyle: the travel, the adventure, how regal Dad looked when he saluted. My father served in the air force for thirty-two years and fought in three wars. Also, as you know, he was a Tuskegee Airman—one of the valiant Black pilots who helped end segregation in the armed services and fascism overseas. Their leadership paved the way for the civil rights movement.

My father's work took us all over the globe, from the rich cultural landscape of Izmir, Turkey, to Arizona, Iowa, Alabama, and Ohio—all right here in the home of the brave. So for most of my childhood, relocating was the norm. That changed in 1969, when we moved to Biloxi, Mississippi, for my father's final assignment. Dad, who began his career as a pre-aviation cadet private, retired in Biloxi as a full colonel in 1975. He and my mother loved the area so much they adopted the Gulf Coast as our new home.

I was fifteen when we settled in the Pass, and I was

nervous ahead of the transition there. I'd be the new kid in a school where my classmates had known one another essentially since birth, which folks do in a small town. All I could think was, *How will I fit in?*

My childhood had prepared me with a playbook. Every few years, my father had been transferred to a different military base, so I'd grown accustomed to making new friends. That skill came in handy when I entered Pass Christian High, but it also helped that many students and teachers were so kind to me. (A special thank-you to my classmate Loretta Wimbley, for coming to the rescue of a tall, pigtailed newbie.) As my mom would often shake her head and say, "All that needless worry..." It dawned on me then that in conquering fear, our own journeys are the best points of reference.

The nerves showed up for me again when I left home for college, my first time on my own. I can't recall ever before spending the night anyplace without a family member close by. When I was in grade school, slumber parties were all the rage, and while we hosted them, my folks wouldn't allow me to sleep over at my classmates' houses. "You never know what goes on in someone else's home," my folks would say. So when Mom and Dad moved me into my dorm room, I wailed myself to sleep that night.

When I awakened, I saw a book on my nightstand. Mom had left me a copy of *Streams in the Desert*, the devotional my family has read for generations. Glimpsing the volume immediately made me feel connected with my folks. They wouldn't have left me if they weren't sure I'd be safe, especially my mother. Years later, Dad told me Momma cried all the way home. She begged him to go back and get me, but he knew if he did, I would've jumped right back in the car with them! Daddy was strong for both of us, a lesson that eventually helped me face cancer. As I trembled my way through that terrifying period, I kept hearing, "You're so brave!" when I felt anything but daring. I did, however, focus on the fight, not the fright—another truism I cling to. And yet when weariness engulfed me, I borrowed the strength of my loved ones.

My mother, Rock of Gibraltar that she was, never preached fearlessness, but she exhibited it. For Christmas 2003, I offered my family a gift: a trip to South Africa, birthplace of the hero Nelson Mandela. For years we'd dreamed of visiting but hadn't. (My tour with President Clinton was later.) Ahead of our vacation, Mom's arthritis made walking long distances a challenge for her. We knew it'd be difficult for her to travel in that condition. So she saw doctor after doctor and even began working with a physical therapist. No improvement. At one point, she became so discouraged that she doubted she'd be able to go. That's when her therapist asked her point-blank, "Mrs. Roberts, do you *want* to be well?"

That exchange prompted an epiphany. My mother, a woman of deep faith, drew from her well of fortitude. In that instant, she decided that, yes, she wanted to recover—that she wouldn't allow her arthritis to keep her from sharing a wonderful memory with her family. And then a miracle happened: She steadily progressed. And Momma was right there with us during every magical step of our two weeks in South Africa that spring: through the streets of Joburg, along the byways of Cape Town, even climbing into a jeep for our safari! And on the morning we boarded the ferry to Robben Island—where Mr. Mandela, the ultimate profile in courage, was confined to a seven-by-nine-foot concrete cell for eighteen years—my parents strode onto that boat looking like African royalty. Mom had on her leopard-skin hat, while Dad was sporting a leather coat.

That moment was captured in the photo that now greets me when I enter my apartment. There are my folks, glowing and majestic, with my mother a walking example. Her determination, on that journey and beyond, is the basis for a powerful question: Do you want it more than you fear it? It's what I now ask myself whenever trepidation makes a house call.

For Momma, the heartache of possibly missing the motherland alongside her tribe became greater than the pain of pushing through therapy. Therein lies the tipping point for all change: We have to yearn, for whatever it is we desire, strongly enough to endure the discomfort in working toward it. That is, in part, what renowned civil rights activist Rosa Parks meant when she said this: "I have learned over the years that when one's mind is made up, this diminishes fear."[2] And in 1955, her boldness aboard a Montgomery, Alabama, bus irrevocably altered the world's course. By taking a seat, Ms. Rosa made a stand and set fear back on its heels. She also left humanity with a template for temerity.

Faith isn't simply the anchor I reach for in terrifying moments. It has become my living testimony. It has walked by my side through the valley of chemo. It has steadied me through quivering lips, through spells of anguish and bouts of desperation. It has carried this lanky Black girl from small-town Mississippi to the halls of the White House, with an up-close view of history. We don't have to be strong to tiptoe out on faith, or be brave to muster courage. Sometimes we just need to attempt the shot, even with our knees shaking.

Chapter 8

Your Tribe Determines Your Vibe

If you hang out with chickens, you're going to cluck; and if you hang out with eagles, you're going to fly.

—*Steve Maraboli*

I'm blessed in the tribe department. I was so close to a couple of my high school basketball teammates, Cheryl and Luella, that we began calling ourselves the True Blues. The name stuck, and so has our tight bond. Then there are my long-standing college connections (#LionUp, Southeastern alums!), as well as the amazing BFFs who share my world now. I'm grateful for the incredible friends who've crossed my path, because in doing so, they've lit it.

"Life is partly what we make it," said Chinese philosopher Dr. Tehyi Hsieh, "and partly what it is made by the friends we choose"[1]—his point being that we should choose carefully. Our vibe does much of the picking for us. You and I are living, breathing magnets, energy fields capable of drawing others toward us. We're also sensors. Ever notice how, after a conversation with one person, you feel lighter and freer, while an exchange with someone else clenches your jaw? That's your body's way of indicating the type of vibe exchanged, a visceral thumbs-up or thumbs-down.

Some call that energy a life force. Others call it a spirit. No matter what we name it, it's undeniably forceful, so much so that it can alter our trajectory in life. We become not just what we believe and think about. We also mirror those we dine with, dance with, pray with, cry with, and rub shoulders with most regularly. Your tribe determines your vibe, and vice versa.

Brighter by the day—that's our goal. Our journey there winds through the land of consciousness. We've got to become aware of the energy we emit—like attracts like—as well as the folks we bring close. In my own life, I'm drawn to what author Joyce Landorf Heatherley called "balcony people"[2]—those who high-five us in the good times, love us when we're doubled over, and add sunshine to even the dreariest afternoons. That's in contrast to "basement people," those who are generally critical. Discouraging. Wear *Bah! Humbug!* on their brows. All of us can be balcony or basement people at any given time, but I seek out those uplifting people who frequent the gallery.

By *uplifting*, I don't mean fake. My tribe members aren't yes people; they're real people. They call me out on things. "You're one hundred percent perfect," said no one ever in my crew. Like many, I have my cellar moments. They usually come when I'm overwhelmed or sleep-deprived, running from coast to coast. I periodically get snippy with those I love, the ones who've made me safe enough to be my full self, clapbacks and all. But we can initiate hard conversations with one another. I try to listen more than I speak. And through all of our exchanges runs a river of positivity, a sense that, even when one of us is dead wrong, the spirit of the feedback is right. You can keep things authentic and still keep them constructive. I insist on that.

That's correct: No Debbie Downers allowed in my orbit, because when we surround ourselves with dark energy, we absorb it. "I'm convinced that the negative has power," the wise Maya Angelou once told Oprah Winfrey. "And if you allow it to perch in your house, in your mind, in your life, it can take you over. Those negative words climb into the woodwork, into the furniture, and the next thing you know, they're on your skin. A negative statement is a poison."[3]

My girlfriend, Amber, can attest. Back when she was working as a massage therapist, she'd occasionally have a client with strong basement energy. "I know you're paying me well," she'd politely say, "but I'll need to recommend someone else for you to work with." The negative vibe had become an albatross.

Not that my tribe and I are temperamentally homogeneous, or exactly alike in any regard. We come from different walks of life, and we're scattered all over the country: Lois Ann in Nevada, Julie in Texas, Nancy in Louisiana, Beth and Beth Jr. in Georgia, Tara in New Hampshire, Jo in Maine. Carol and our newbies, Barbara and Bill, are right down the road from Amber and me in Connecticut. Our professions run the range. One pal is a therapist. (We love having Linda, or Dr. B, as we affectionately call her, among us...She keeps our heads on straight!) A couple of friends have leapt into their second acts: Kim went back to school at midlife to pursue her dream career as a university athletic director—love that. Linda's wife, Scarlett, stepped down from an executive position and started her own business in Arizona...The desert landscape was calling her name.

Every one of my tribe members—and I say this with my palm pressed over my heart in profound gratitude—walked with me through the bleak corridor of cancer. Michelle made Cajun dishes for me. All of them ripped back and forth across the country to see me through hellish rounds of chemo. They had my back and also rubbed it; they held me as I wept.

Not every one of these friends runs naturally sunny, and they don't need to. Positivity comes in various shapes and sizes. It can manifest as trustworthiness. Encouragement. Honesty. Acceptance. Whatever its form, it elevates.

Look around your life. Who's in your inner circle,

and routinely in your ear? And, more to the point, how do you feel when you're with your crew, as well as after you've hugged them goodbye? Does a sweet scent linger or an unpleasant one? Do you light up or groan when you notice a friend's name appear on caller ID?

Here's a shortcut to assessing vibe: Your feelings are an accurate barometer. A true blue, however he or she shows up, only wants the best for you. You can sense that. You know, deep down, when someone is jealous of you, secretly resents you, or keeps you close because misery loves a road dog. And it's easy to spot the scorekeepers, the guilt-trippers ("Wow, I haven't heard from you in *weeks*..."), and the general manipulators. Pay attention to your instincts, because seldom, if ever, do they stammer. And once you've determined the vibe in your tribe, you might decide to make some cuts.

Even just a trim can be excruciating. Last year, I began contemplating whether to continue with a friendship, one that goes way back. And that's the thing: When you have a long shared history with someone, with fond memories to show for it, it's hard to back away. I value and appreciate longevity; I come from a family where it's prized. My parents were married for more than five decades. Amber and I have been together for nearly twenty years. I've known most of my tribe for eons. But this one friend, long-standing as she is, has grown increasingly toxic. Truthfully, I've tolerated her negativity for a while, but our changing times have thrust it onto center stage. I've been avoiding the conversation I need to have, mostly because I know it'll hurt.

So you're not alone in your struggle to brighten up your corner, nor do any of us think we're better than those we distance ourselves from. Every human being has inherent worth, even if a different vibration. Still, we honor our truth when we actually speak it: "I love you, but this isn't working for me, and I need to protect my well-being."

To navigate any tough situation, be it letting go of a friendship or changing a habit, we have to get leverage on ourselves, the same way my dear mother did before our South Africa trip. Remember: When the pain of whatever we're experiencing becomes more intense than the ache we'd feel in ending it, that's when we find the wherewithal to act. Let's be patient with ourselves while we get there.

What impacts our vibe more than anything? How we speak to ourselves. The thoughts we entertain or dismiss. The experiences we brood over or choose to move on from. We have to guard our headspace ever so fiercely, and also tune in to what our hunches are telling us. I love this insight often attributed to the Dalai Lama: "When you talk, you are only repeating what you already know. But if you listen, you may learn something new."[4] It reminds me that when I sit quietly, there's something to be discovered, even about myself. It's in the silence of the mornings, as the sun yawns awake, that I most often hear my whispers, those nudges about whether to go left or right. We usually have our own answers. We just have to settle down long enough to hear them.

We also have to find ways to celebrate our besties, because what's the point of having friends if we don't *enjoy* them? We'd all talked about going to Hawaii "one day," and after I'd completed chemo, I made that dream a day-one priority. I wanted to thank my adopted family for standing by me as closely as the one I was born into has. I wanted to say—not in words, but in time spent—"I wouldn't have made it through without you." So in 2013, we packed our swimsuits and headed for Maui, land of pristine beaches and lush forests. We all stayed in one big house, our laughter rising to the rafters, our spirits soaking up the joy.

That vacation was the gift that kept on giving, because since then, we've upped our travel game. We don't have to be going anyplace fancy. We'll just call each other and say, "Hey, I'll be in your region. Do you want to meet in so-and-so state between us?" It's not about fanfare, but just about being together. Because when we gather with balcony people, their presence alone lifts us higher.

Chapter 9

Get Ready for Your Suddenly

I believe in hard work. It keeps the wrinkles out of the mind and spirit.

—*Helena Rubenstein,* My Life for Beauty

Long before I was a *GMA* anchor, I was a young reporter with one good blue skirt. On the day I strode in to meet Alan Griggs, then news director at WSMV in Nashville, I paired that staple with two others: a crisp white cotton shirt, which I'd ironed the life out of, and black pumps. You couldn't have told me I wasn't sharp, but someone should've told me to lose the ratty briefcase. It was nearly empty anyhow, with just one or two papers inside, but it pulled together my little dress-for-success power ensemble. "Thanks for coming by," said Alan, his eyes dancing as he stroked his beard. "What brings you to the area?"

In a word, gumption. I'd started in sportscasting right out of college, and after that $5.50-an-hour half gig in Hattiesburg, I'd leapfrogged my way over to Biloxi. I'd learned plenty in both places but was itching to graduate to a larger market, and also to put more distance between the poverty line and my paycheck. So in 1986, a couple of years into my career, I got creative. My parents, who traveled often on church business, had agreed to give me a heads-up on where they'd be going so I could hitch a ride. My plan: to make myself visible on the network scene.

So when Dad and Mom mentioned that their next stop was Opryland, I contacted three news directors in nearby Nashville and requested meetings. It wouldn't cost them a nickel, I explained, since I'd be staying with my folks. And I wasn't asking for a job; I simply wanted my résumé tape critiqued, and then a brief chat. Alan, God bless that man, was the only one who rang me back.

On the afternoon of my visit, we hit it off instantly. He watched my tape and saw potential in my on-camera presence. He promised to stay in touch, and then did. Nine months later, his pledge turned into a job. And, let me tell you, Alan didn't just hire me. He truly believed in me. In addition to helping me become a better journalist, he counseled me on finances. I'll always remember receiving my first Christmas bonus. It wasn't much, but it was more than I'd ever gotten at once. Alan felt bad that the station didn't offer a retirement plan, and he suggested ways I could begin setting aside money, investing for my future. I'll always be incredibly grateful to him.

Alan and I are now friends, and we still laugh about the day I sashayed in, with my scruffy attaché and my big hair. He mercifully looked past both to spot an enterprising reporter, one with an extra helping of initiative. I had no Ivy League degree or fancy credentials, but I'd nonetheless managed to wedge my pump into a top-thirty market.

What journalist, just two years out of university, cold-calls a Peabody Award–winning station and asks for a sit-down? One who's hungry. One who's been filming her own reports with a clunky one-armed-bandit camcorder, and then having her anchorwoman sister, Sally-Ann, critique them. One who's practiced pronouncing her *e*'s and *i*'s ad nauseam, after her stickler-for-diction momma tells her they're sounding lazy on air. And one who's learned that so-called overnight success comes one deliberate, gutsy move at a time.

Getting ready for my suddenly: In the decade that brought us shoulder pads and MTV, that's what I was doing. By the time I broke into broadcasting, the principle was second nature to me. I'd learned it in basketball, tennis, bowling—you name it—because as a student athlete, I took that Title IX ruling and sprinted down the field with it. My coaches drilled the idea into us: Position yourself to score. Grabbing rebounds, for instance, doesn't just happen. You've got to place yourself between your opponent and the basket so you can recover the ball the moment a shot goes wonky. In tennis, a strong forehand is all in the preparation: aligning your hips and upper body to move in concert with the racket. Positioning is what leads to triumph. Proximity is what lends power.

As it goes on the Grand Slam courts, so it goes in life. We can wish and daydream on an endless loop, but if we're going to lob our goals over into the "done" column, we have to, first of all, show up. Then, once we're actually in the match, it's time to strategize—about when to move, how to seize on openings, and how best to plant our feet. Because to send a sure winner flying over that net, a champion has to be situated for it. One shot at a time, through set after set, he or she must *create* the conditions for victory.

At birth, we're not given a magic wand, but we are handed a menu of options. As our years whir by—more and more swiftly, it seems for me—will we stagnate on the sidelines or take bold, tactical action? "The future depends on what we do in the present," the great Mahatma Gandhi has been quoted as saying.[1] Our lives are the sum total of our thoughts and habits, and that ultimately adds up to our destiny.

We cannot control what events will arise, as the last few years have reminded us. And yet we do have a say in our positioning—whether we'll walk, crawl, shuffle, or slide our way through circumstances—and I hope you'll join my co-anchor Michael Strahan in standing prepared. "I don't *get* ready," I've heard my dear friend say with a chuckle. "I *stay* ready." Hear, hear, No. 92! A power posture, as he so well knows, can become a long-term norm.

My "suddenly" began well before I arrived at *GMA*. In the mid-1990s, while I was still anchoring ESPN's *SportsCenter*, I was offered a second hosting gig, on ABC's *Wide World of Sports*. (ESPN and ABC are part of the same corporate family.) The new role brought me into the ABC studios on weekends. The team liked my on-air work, and, in time, the *GMA* execs asked me to file sports stories.

Proximity may be power, but few things are more potent than a task well done. I share that with my mentees these days: Whether you're serving tea or serving as VP, pour your passion into it. Today's masterful execution attracts tomorrow's opportunity... Your excellent work will run its mouth all over town.

Though I had a toe in the *GMA* door, I was still an infrequent contributor. I love the advice my then agent gave me. "Be seen," he said. "Even if you don't have a story to file, even if you aren't on the clock, hang around the office and you might get an assignment." His advice paid off. I was eventually given the chance to cohost *GMA* on Sundays. (Thank you, Willow Bay, for speaking up for me!) Next thing I knew, in 2005, I was joining two legends, Diane Sawyer and Charlie Gibson, in saying "Good morning, America." Visibility matters.

So does committing a smart plan to paper. My former *GMA* intern Jade understands this. First of all, she set herself apart by stopping to see me near the end of her internship... Hello, visibility. I'd been impressed with her work, so when an opening arose as social media director, I recommended her. Months later, I was prepping for an assignment to cover the Special Olympics in Abu Dhabi. Every staffer and his or her momma was trying to get onto that big trip. Instead of begging and boondoggling, Jade marched into my office with a full proposal—of how she could leverage our social media while in the United Arab Emirates. Jade, in fact, usually puts her ideas in writing. It's one reason

I'm glad she was hired. Positioning yourself to take the first shot is one thing. But a consistently superb performance, hoop after hoop, is what keeps you in the contest.

I sometimes miss the phase Jade and my other young, dynamic staffers, Reni, Nicole, and Danielle are navigating—the excitement that comes with that early hustle, the breathlessness and the wondering, *Will I make it?* I was at four different stations in seven years, and I look back fondly on that stage.

Though I'm in a much different place in my career now—and arms raised to heaven for this season—I stay on the lookout for new ways to grow... always grateful, never content. I'm constantly moving my goalposts farther back so I have to stretch in order to score.

These days, I challenge myself by running Rock'n Robin Productions, the broadcast and digital media company I began in 2014. Our mission is clear: to inform, uplift, enlighten, and entertain—all four at once when we can. I don't just take the calls; I also make them. I'm out there pitching content all the time, because, as Babe Ruth noted, you've got to strike out hundreds of times to get a single home run. It can be humbling to hear the word *no* again, to reset and have to fine-tune my proposals. But it's all part of positioning my company for good things to happen, the way I did back when I donned that navy pencil skirt.

This isn't only about career and on-court strides; the idea applies broadly. Repetition is the mother of skill, and what we rehearse, we slowly become. When my grandma Sally rose daily at dawn for her quiet time, she was embracing a form of mindfulness. She was learning to dim the distractions of our world and hear the still, small voice of the Spirit. She was training for calm. Show me someone who seems unflappable amid calamity, and I'll show you a person who likely practices some kind of solitude, who sits alone for stretches.

Remember, optimism is a muscle that gets stronger with use, the key word being *use*. And here's another word for you: *discipline*, as in honoring the promise we've made to ourselves that we'll look for the bright side. We stay on the positive path by shifting our gaze sunward a little at a time, until all we see is the horizon.

Chapter 10

Lighter by the Day

You can't go back and make a new start,
but you can start right now and make a
brand new ending.

—James R. Sherman

Of the many moving interviews I've done over my career, one in particular touched me deeply. As part of my work with ABC's *20/20*, I sat down with Marietta Jaeger Lane, a mom enduring the unimaginable. In the summer of 1973, Marietta and her then husband, Bill, had taken their five children on a family camping trip in Montana. On the first stop of their adventure, Marietta had awakened to horror: Susie, her youngest child, was missing; the tent where her daughter was sleeping had been cut open. Intense search-and-rescue efforts yielded no clues. "I was just ravaged with hatred and a desire for revenge," Marietta later told ABC. If she'd had the chance, she felt like she could've killed the abductor, she said—"with my bare hands and a smile on my face."

In 2000, I flew to Montana to sit down with the mother, and her account heartens me to this day. In the months after the abduction, Marietta, reared as a Roman Catholic, made a surprising choice. While still holding out hope that she'd reunite with her child, Marietta had moved from understandable fury to profound forgiveness. "I knew that hatred wasn't healthy, that it would obsess and consume me," she told me. "Were I to give in to that kind of mindset, it would be my undoing. It's not to say that it was an easy realization, because I felt absolutely justified. I had every right to feel how I did."

On the one-year anniversary of Susie's disappearance, Marietta mentioned in press reports that she'd forgiven the abductor. Soon after, she received a chilling phone call.

The man on the line identified himself as Susie's kidnapper. He'd rung to taunt her, but Marietta's compassionate response stunned him. "I've been praying for you ever since you took her," she said calmly. She then asked him how he was doing and whether she could help. "I genuinely wanted to reach him," she said. "I don't think he was expecting that. And I really meant it with all my heart."

The FBI, who'd anticipated that the kidnapper might contact Marietta, recorded Marietta's long talk with the man. Though the call wasn't successfully traced, the conversation revealed clues that helped identify a suspect, a man who'd been detained in connection with other crimes. He fit the psychological profile the FBI had pieced together.

Still, investigators needed irrefutable evidence. So they arranged for Marietta to meet in person with the alleged abductor, at which time he confessed to snatching and murdering Susie. Soon after, he took his own life.

Marietta not only found closure through a radical act of forgiveness, but she also extended that healing by reaching out to the man's mom. "Together we were able to grieve as mothers who had lost their children," she said. "I hoped that it would help her to know that I had forgiven him."

Marietta has made her mess her message by advocating against the death penalty, as well as standing beside families who've lost loved ones to heinous crimes. Says Marietta: "Those victims who will not relinquish a vindictive mindset end up giving the offender another victim—themselves."

Years after I talked with Marietta, I remain inspired by her ability to exonerate someone who completely upended her family. I've never forgotten the recording she played for me of the man's icy admission on the phone that day: "I'm the one who took your daughter," he breathed. But even when she later stared into the abductor's eyes as he detailed his atrocity, during an admission that might've undone most of us, she was at peace. What a testimony. And what an illustration of the power of clemency.

"How were you able to forgive him?" I recall asking Marietta. "I did it for me," she replied, "not for him." She understood that when we pardon others, it is ourselves we let off the hook. It eases our load and lifts our spirits. It frees us up to get on with the work we're here to do.

Judge Esther Salas also knows that. I sat down with Esther, the first Latina US district court judge in New Jersey, a few months after her dear son, Daniel, was killed in their home in 2020, and her husband, Mark, was seriously injured. The attacker, a self-described "anti-feminist," had intended to assassinate Judge Salas. He hated that she was a judge, and a Latina one at that.

During our conversation, Esther spoke lovingly of her son and said she'd forgiven the murderer. "Hate is heavy," she told me. "Love is light."

Forgiveness isn't about moving on, as Esther told me one year after her blow. It's about moving *forward*. When you let go of a hurt, you're not somehow condoning cruel behavior. Rather, you're insisting on your own liberation. You're recognizing resentment as a ball and chain, and deciding to lay it aside. Coretta Scott King expressed it this way: "Hate is too great a burden to bear. It injures the hater more than it injures the hated."[1] Forgiveness, conversely, is a salt bath for the soul.

None of this means we should dismiss trauma and its residual impact on our brains and bodies. The process of forgiveness—because, yes, it is a *process*, a heart-set we commit to time and again—often happens in the context of deep therapeutic work.

It should. When we survive a psychological wound caused by a crushing experience, our emotional center must be reset. We're in need of a full cast, a healing overseen by a professional, not simply a proclamation that we've buried the hatchet that battered us.

Forgiveness isn't a substitute for therapy. It's a complement to and possible result of it. Only after we begin unpacking and truly dealing with the crushing experience we had can we start letting go of the hostility attached to our wound. We do so in order to make space, in spiritual terms, since relinquishing animosity frees up room for love to flourish. Spite and light cannot peacefully coexist. When we allow bygones to be bygones, we rush malice out the door and invite joy to stay.

An admirable few can lend mercy to a family member's murderer, as Marietta and Esther did. Yet we can all practice forgiveness in small increments. Maybe someone has stung you with a sharp retort, or another person has ignored your input. Or perhaps a friend has betrayed your trust, or an acquaintance is spreading rumors about you. Consider voicing your feelings with an honest heart-to-heart. Acrimony grows in the shadows, while thrusting it into the daylight cuts off its circulation.

As you're mustering the courage to do so, you can begin by changing your inner dialogue about the person or situation. (When you think of the offender, for instance, decide you won't disparage him or her... You may not yet be ready to acquit, but you're at least committing to doing no harm.) That's how you become what psychologist Robert Enright calls "forgivingly fit"[2]—you slowly exercise the muscle of granting amnesty.

As close as I am with my family, we've had to work that muscle. An annoyance once arose that could have damaged our connection. My beloved grandma Sally, my mother's mom, passed away in 1991. Following her homegoing service in Ohio, Mom gathered with my siblings and me at Grandma Sally's modest apartment, where a few of her treasured keepsakes remained. "Take whatever items you'd like," Mom encouraged us. "She'd want you to have them."

I first chose my grandmother's dog-eared, highlighted copy of *Streams in the Desert*, our family's cherished devotional. Soon after, Sally-Ann and I disagreed over who should have one of my grandmother's other belongings. A heated back-and-forth followed.

On the long car ride home from Ohio to Mississippi, the irritation was palpable. None of us said a word for the entire trip. Butch dropped me off at my parents' house in the Pass and continued on to New Orleans with the others. I got out of the car, vowing I'd never speak to Sally-Ann again . . . That's just how angry I was.

I'm shaking my head and chuckling as I write this, because the whole thing seems so silly now. But in that moment, I was hot.

Minutes after I'd entered the house, the phone rang. It was my brother. He'd stopped at a pay phone. (Remember those, in the years before cells?)

"Families split up over this kind of thing, Robin," he said. He refused to let another moment pass before my sister and I reconciled.

He put Sally-Ann on the phone, and we muttered our apologies. I don't think either of us was really ready to patch things up, but we knew it was best. So did Butch. He'd witnessed how a seemingly trivial dispute could harden into a deep-rooted bitterness—one capable of destroying a tribe.

Our polarized times are fraught with tensions that can wreak havoc in our relationships. Battle lines have been drawn over everything from mask wearing and vaccination to political and social beliefs. There are family members and friends no longer speaking to one another. Some will reunite, others never will. Here's what my wise brother understood: Even a minor irritation, if left unaddressed, clogs our spiritual pores. Then at the moment when we most crave connection, the pathway to that support has been blocked.

Had Butch not intervened that day, and had my sister and I been unwilling to mend fences, would

Sally-Ann have been there for me years later when I desperately needed her to save my life? I shudder at the potential outcome if we hadn't quickly cleared the air. In the years since that incident, I've held tight to the lesson: Keep short accounts. Butch didn't want us to go to sleep angry, because one day of seething could have easily turned into a decade.

My sister and I actually laugh about the whole thing now. A week after our dust-up, Sally-Ann came to my parents' house and gave me a big hug. With that embrace, we chose forgiveness.

Lightening our loads, brightening our days—that's at the heart of this book's intention. It's rising above our encumbrances, soaring toward our best lives, and finding the good in our goodbyes. Make this the year you turn the page on a grievance. Wave your white flag in surrender. Not because someone else deserves emancipation, but because you do. Let yourself off that hot seat you're on and relax your shoulders.

Chapter 11

God's Delays Are Not His Denials

The two most powerful warriors are patience and time.

—Leo Tolstoy

God has three answers to prayer. The first is *Yes,* that approving nod that prompts a hallelujah dance. The second is *Not yet,* a holding pattern that often looks more like a red light than a yellow one. And the third is, *I have something better in mind for you*—the reply heaven specializes in. Spotting a *Yes* is easy. Less simple is knowing when you're standing in a *Hold that thought* or a *Stay tuned for something greater.* I can testify.

During my last days of college, I got well acquainted with *Not yet.* It showed up as a rejection letter... Actually, enough of them to paper a den. In step with my plan to break into sports broadcasting at the JV level, I'd flooded small stations with my résumé tape. Many of my classmates had aimed for top markets—New York, LA, Chicago—but I had taken a different approach.

Why? Because as Gwen Guthrie once sang, "You

got to have a j-o-b if you wanna be with me"—and I had neither a j-o-b nor any prospects for one. While I'm all about dreaming in color, I'm also about staying in the black. So as others set their sights on the Big Dipper, I fixed mine on its little sis.

Crickets—that's what I heard back from most of the places I wrote to. For every denial I received, dozens of stations never bothered to respond. When I did get an answer, my tape came boomeranging back mere days after I'd submitted it. *Couldn't they have held it for a week,* I wondered, *so I'd think they'd actually considered me?*

Amid my disappointment, I let my fingers do the walking, looking up and calling one news director after the next. No one would even *talk* to me. The word *defeated* doesn't quite capture the extent of my discouragement. The surge of rejections made me second-guess my abilities. *Am I good enough?*

I did get nibbles—most notably from WLOX in Biloxi—but all were in news, not sportscasting. At one point, I felt so dejected I thought, *Maybe*

I should just take a news anchor position and be satisfied. That's when WDAM in Hattiesburg—the same station where my sister Sally-Ann got her start in television—rang with the part-time offer I jumped at. And then, a year later, heaven finally cleared its throat. Biloxi circled back with an opening in the sports department. God's delays are not His denials.

But memory is a funny thing. Because by the time I'd grown antsy to move to a larger market, spiritual amnesia had set in. Once again, I sent out my tapes, more widely this time: Houston, Baton Rouge, New Orleans. And once again, my mailbox filled with so many nos I lost count.

I slid down into an emotional spiral, one steeper than the previous one. The first time, I'd been a bright shade of green right out of university, with one lonely little position, though a great one, as assistant news director and deejay at that country music station. But now, I'd held down two j-o-bs, learned to research every square inch of my stories, scoured three newspapers a day, done my homework and my time. I'd used the delay as an opportunity to improve, to hone my writing and interview techniques.

I knew I had a lot to offer. The rejection letters littering my kitchen counter signaled otherwise. I'd seen this movie two years earlier, and yet I'd somehow forgotten how it ended.

We pray for what we want and . . . nada. For weeks, months, or sometimes decades, we understandably assume heaven has a CLOSED sign on its front gate. But then we realize, as I did in 1986, that God has had His own agenda all along, on a schedule we hadn't glimpsed. The creator of time is not on our clock. He doesn't even own a wristwatch. In His grand plan, in His vision extending far beyond my limited one, He knew I needed to be at WSMV in Nashville. A place where I'd be nurtured. A station where Alan Griggs would mold and mentor me.

The Almighty also knew I needed to turn down ESPN's first offer, the one everybody thought I was nuts to let slip away. Yes, I'm the one who pressed that pause button, but my finger was divinely guided.

The Spirit whispered, through my instincts, that I wasn't ready for prime time.

Recently on Zoom, I was speaking to a group of young journalists. "How did you know not to take the job?" one asked. I didn't capital *K* know anything for sure, but I did know myself and I followed my inclination. Still, I had my doubts about how things would work out. I might look like a genius now for passing up the job, but the choice was still a leap. When we're facing a decisive moment, we have no crystal ball. That's why faith is called faith, what Hebrews 11:1 describes as "confidence in what we hope for and assurance about what we do not see."

I had no certainty that I'd get another chance at ESPN, but when I did, the scene had changed in my favor. John A. Walsh, who'd recently been brought in as managing editor at *SportsCenter*, became my Alan. What I thought had been a halt or a nay was now looking more like a love note from God: *I have something better in mind for you.*

And, boy, did He. Fast-forward to the late 1990s,

when I was earning my wings as an occasional *GMA* contributor. My agent called me with good news. "The executive producer wants to make you a regular contributor," he told me. Cue the hula dance. I was so thrilled that I maybe bragged a little about getting this sweet gig. Weeks later, I strutted into the EP's office thinking he was going to make it official: I was a rising star at *GMA*.

Problem was, a new sheriff had come to town. The EP who'd wanted to promote me was out, and he'd been replaced by one who informed me he was "going in a different direction." *Ouch.* When you strut, you stumble, as Momma said, and I stumbled my tail right out of that office. But that's not how the story ends. The new EP didn't last long, nor did the person he hired instead of me. Often, what we call "rejection" is God's protection—a spin on *Stick with me, child, this train is going someplace else.* And years later, in 2005, I got off at the stop called "*GMA* co-anchor."

The Father's plan can come packaged as your plan: the remix. That was the case with my athletic aspirations, because, let's be honest, I once dreamed of going pro, but pragmatism made me keep that goal quiet for a time. Then after a career day in sixth grade, I went home and announced to my mother, "I'm going to be a physical education teacher, because that's all you can do as a woman who loves sports." Mom, who could sniff out baloney from a town away, looked me square in the eyes and said, "You are copping out. That's not what you want to do. I know you, child."

Whoo! Here I'd thought Mom would be so pleased to have me follow in her footsteps as an educator, and she instead encouraged me to own my dream, to dance with it, to invite it to stay. For the first time in my childhood, I thought, *Okay, so I'm not supposed to settle.* Still, I struggled over my direction. I didn't have the patience for coaching, which seemed like one of the only viable paths into a profession in sports for women.

I once said to my dad, "People are asking me what I want be one day."

A smile spread over his face. "Tell them you want to be kind," he said.

That took away the pressure but didn't solve the riddle: What does a very tall girl from a very small town grow up to do with her life? Meanwhile, I continued playing nearly every sport known to womankind. Oh, and did I mention I was the state bowling champion in Mississippi when I was twelve? Tennis, though, was my first love. I spent hours at a small park in our town, practicing my forehand on the courts as I imagined one day competing at Wimbledon. I could see myself curtsying to the royal box, taking to the court in my fresh whites, waving as the crowd roared. In eighth grade—thanks to my height—I added basketball to my lineup of sports loves. I was pretty good, too, when I look back on it... The older I got, the better I was.

In my high school, I became the first basketball player in years to make it to All-State. I also went to the state high school tennis tournament with my mixed doubles partner, Pat Barnes. You should've seen our matching outfits, which we purchased at T.J. Maxx! At SLU, I graduated as the Lady Lions' third-highest scorer and rebounder, but who's counting? Yet, to have any real shot at a professional career, there's this little thing you need called *ability*—as in more than I had.

It was my sister Sally-Ann—eight years older and already working as a news anchor in New Orleans—who steered me toward sportscasting. And once I took that right turn, I did not look back. I did occasionally feel a wistfulness for my childhood aspiration—not a sigh of regret but one of joy, with a twinkle in my eye and a smile on my face. No matter how successful you are, you still cherish the dreams of your early years, still think back on the road not taken.

The Master may not don a Seiko, but He does have a sense of humor. I did make it to the All England Club, but as a reporter/anchor for ESPN. Yes, I held a microphone instead of a racket, but I still thought, *Wimbledon—check!* We can get so fixated on a specific request that we're blinded to the blessings around us. Rigidity folds its arms over its chest, closes itself off to the world. Flexibility, by contrast, has a wide embrace, welcoming *Not yets* and remixes as answers to prayer. Stay open. We may think heaven is hard of hearing, when in fact, it's just busy redirecting our route. We're quick to thank God for the open doors. I also thank Him for the closed ones.

Chapter 12

Make Your Mess Your Message

As we work to create light for others
we naturally light our own way.

—Mary Anne Radmacher

Among my mother's wealth of mommyisms, two reign supreme. The first is the one she shared with me in 2007, after I discovered a lump in my right breast. My eyes, my brow, my entire disposition whispered the question that surfaces in despair: *Why is this happening to me?* Mom, with compassion on her face and warmth in her tone, said, "Honey, everybody's got something"—words that became my anchor.

Throughout my life, Mom spoke a second truth, related to the first. When scrapes and heartaches arose, she'd say, "Make your mess your message—you're not the only one." My suffering wasn't unique, she understood, no more significant than anyone's. My choice was whether to brood and fold inward or turn my pain into purpose. We may not ever fully understand why catastrophe has befallen us, and that's okay. Our job isn't to comprehend it. It's to redeem it for good.

Wherever I am in the world, folks come up to me and utter some version of those two mantras. "Make your mess your message," they'll call out, a shorthand for connection, their way of saying, *I'm with you. I see you. We're all in the same place.* Their "messes," their "somethings," run the gamut. Loss of family and close friends. Divorce. Terminal illness. Bankruptcy. Unemployment. Fill in the blank with your mess. As Mom so often reminded me, tragedy is just part of living. When we languish in self-pity for years at a time, we miss what hardship has to teach us. As much as we savor the mountaintop moments, the miseries are what refine us.

I love the Robert Browning Hamilton poem Mom used to share with me when I'd had a rough day. "'I walked a mile with Pleasure,'" she'd recite. "'She chattered all the way; but left me none the wiser for all she had to say. I walked a mile with Sorrow; and ne'er a word said she; but, oh, the things I learned from her; when Sorrow walked with me.'"[1] Crisis is our best teacher. Growth is the lesson. Service to others is how we pay it forward. And we don't need a bullhorn or a stage to make our message heard. All we need is a desire to bring light to our one corner.

"What's your 'mess' these days?" a friend recently asked me. I had to stop and really think about that. Cancer has long been my fallback answer, a mess with a clear message: Early detection increases your chances of survival. Schedule your mammogram appointment today. In 2012, five years after I thought I'd won the battle, my "mess" became MDS. I went on a campaign to get people signed up in the bone marrow registry; asked them to donate and make research possible; and invited them to take part in clinical trials, as I did along with Sally-Ann, the dear sister who saved my life. Thousands responded.

But here, in the autumn of my life, I don't have a "mess." When you've battled The Big C twice and you're still standing, that ain't no mess; it's a gift. In place of a war wound, I have a passageway—a transition to a new season. It's called *aging.* It's uncertain. It's vulnerable. It's, at turns, surprising and hilarious. And my message, as I brave this path, is that longevity is to be celebrated.

When Momma was in the winter of her life, we kids would tease her about her bifocals. She always had them perched on top of her head, yet half the time, she couldn't find them. "Oh, you just wait!" she'd say. "Your day is coming." How right she was. These bodies of ours, they change for certain, and mine is no exception. Sometimes when I'm getting out of the shower, I catch a glimpse of myself in the mirror and wonder, *Ooh, who's that?*

The constant Zooming during the shutdown didn't help. There I'd be, carrying on business in the most unusual of ways—it's strange to talk with others while looking at yourself!—and I'd catch myself thinking, *What's going on with my neck?* Black may not crack, but it does fold and droop, sometimes down to your knees. And though I'm still in good shape, thanks to my Peloton, silver hairs are sprouting up in places where they just aren't welcome.

And then there are the random aches. In my youth, when I played hoops, no one could drop a shot on me. I was quick as lightning. I recently tried one of my trademark moves on the court, and while my spirit had the will, my body had other plans.

I can't tell you how often I look up to heaven, chuckling, as I say, "I hear you, Momma!" Yes, my friends, fall is upon me. I intend to embrace it with grace and good cheer, and, of course, with my reading glasses close by.

I'll also keep a jacket handy, for the brisk headwinds I sense coming. Invisibility is one. Our culture hails older men as "distinguished," while older women become less and less seen, often wholly disregarded in terms of our smarts. There are a lot of gray-haired male TV anchors, and far fewer female ones. In our society, women get old, whereas men "mature." I still laugh at the way Cher once put it. "I do think that when it comes to aging, we're held to a different standard than men," she observed. "Some guy said to me: 'Don't you think you're too old to sing rock n' roll?' I said: 'You'd better check with Mick Jagger.' "[2] Amen, Cher.

Some years ago on *GMA*, I got a rare close-up

look at that reality. We ran a series called "Walk in Their Shoes." Each anchor chose whose proverbial loafers they'd like to take a stroll in. I picked those of my beloved grandma Sally, who was ninety when she passed in 1991. I wanted to know: How does it feel to move through society as an elderly woman?

The show hired a top-notch Hollywood makeup artist, who spent hours meticulously applying a prosthetic face, one that made me look like I was in my late eighties or early nineties. Braces were placed on my arms and knees to restrict my movement and simulate arthritis. Vaseline was smeared on my eyeglasses so that I'd see the world as someone with glaucoma would. I still have the "after" picture of myself, and I look strikingly like Grandma Sally!

As soon as I exited the studio door, I felt the difference. People usually smile at me on the street, even stop and talk to me. I know, I know: I'm a public person. But still... not a single passerby even looked in my direction. It was as if I didn't exist. In fact, others were clearly trying to *avoid* eye contact with me. It was shocking.

It also made me aware of how seniors, those highly revered in some cultures, are often shunned and discarded in ours. You don't have to be standing on ninety's doorstep to observe the dismissal. A stunningly beautiful colleague of mine once told me she remembers the first time she walked into a room and didn't turn heads. She was then only around age fifty.

Though you may be rippling with vitality, feeling sharper than ever, and still in your prime, you do notice when others shift their perception of you, even if ever so slightly. I'm not all the way into that territory, thank you very much, but I see it starting. I used to be the young'un asked, "Who inspired you to get into broadcasting?" I'm now on the receiving end of such tributes, complete with video clips from back when I rocked that nineties mullet. It's an incredible honor, for sure, but also a recognition—that my career has reached its next milepost.

I'm on the same page with Dolly Parton. Last year, the Tennessee legislature considered a bill to erect a statue of the country music legend on state capitol grounds. Dolly, while appreciative, politely declined the idea. She welcomed the legislature to put up the statue "after I'm gone."[3] I hear you, Dolly. I bet she's feeling what a lot of us do: *Please don't rush me off the stage while I'm still singing.*

Yes, I acknowledge my leaves are changing colors; the Universe sends its nudges. In my True Blue tribe, my friend Luella, a career-long nurse, recently put away her scrubs for good. "Gurrrl, thirty-seven years is plenty," she said. Others around me are likewise transitioning. *Am I supposed to be retiring?* I've thought. While I know I'll pass the baton at some point, I'm still gripping it for now. I've worked hard for my spot in this relay and plan to run every last meter I can.

These years look different for each of us. They're supposed to. There's no one-size-fits-all approach to the harvest and winter seasons, no handbook with all the answers. Age itself is our one true road map, a topographical representation of the dirt roads and highways we've traveled, the terrain we've traversed, and the emotions we've felt through all of it.

The compass on that map's lower right-hand corner points us toward our true north. We know the way. We've always known it. Others have, at times, inspired our eurekas, but the most profound awakenings have come from within.

That is why, unsure as the future may look from here, we have faith in our own readiness. We have confidence in a God who holds tomorrow in His palms. We have, by grace, what we've been blessed with since birth: the opportunity to reinvent ourselves with every sunrise. We're not only brighter, more scintillating, by the day. We're also brimming with hope.

Everybody's got something...in both senses of the phrase, and in keeping with my memoir's title. We have our difficulties and our delights, our agonies and our elations. I remembered that a few years ago, as I was thumbing through a little book entitled *Beach Calling: A Devotional Journal for the Middle Years and Beyond*. The author, Missy Buchanan, is the beautiful woman who helped my mother write her memoir. Missy has since become part of the family; she was even at my sister's wedding and Momma's homegoing service.

Long before I met Missy, she sent me another of her books, *Living with Purpose in a Worn-Out Body.* I realized it wasn't for me, but I thought Mom would like it, so I passed it on to her. Next thing I knew, my mother had Missy on the phone! "I liked the book," she told me, laughing, "so I thought I'd track her down." When it came time for Mom to share her story, Missy drove from her home in Dallas to the Pass to sit down with my mother over gumbo and intimate conversation. It's Missy's calling to make the sages among us feel seen, heard, valued. And something in her beach volume resonated with me.

In one passage, Missy invites us readers to think about a time during childhood when we felt joy. What brought that sense of pleasure, of play, of wonder and curiosity about the world? The first word that popped into my head: *tennis.* When I was a kid, my parents used to have to drag me off the court.

That's how much I loved the sport. When one of the many tennis magazines I subscribed to came in the mail, I'd rush out to the mailbox, grab my treasure, disappear into my bedroom, and relish the content. I read the same articles over and over, so much so that my magazines no longer had covers! And yet, I realized now, I hadn't played tennis consistently since college. That changed soon after I ran across that encouragement in Missy's pages.

Amber and I went on vacation at the end of 2019, and I took a tennis lesson. I can't tell you how good it felt to wrap my fingers around a racket again! It took me back to when I'd dreamed of Wimbledon, when life was bursting with possibilities, when this pigtailed Black girl could do and be anything, when I felt strong and invincible. "I'm going to find an indoor court to play on this winter in New York," I told Amber.

Two months later, COVID-19 arrived and flipped the world's circuit breaker. Still, I made a way. On our weekends in Key West, I found a local tennis court—nothing fancy—where a great instructor,

Paul, hits balls with me. It was a gift from Amber on my sixtieth birthday. She'd asked me what I wanted, and without hesitation, I said, "Tennis lessons." These days, I'm a bit slower than I once was, and my forehand was never that great. It doesn't matter. Just being out there brings me unfiltered happiness. I can't wait to get home to Mississippi and hit some ground strokes on my childhood court. I haven't stepped foot there in decades, but I've now promised myself I'll return.

"We don't stop playing because we grow old," George Bernard Shaw has been credited with saying. "We grow old because we stop playing."[4] By the playwright's definition, the young don't have an exclusive on vibrancy; you and I can cultivate it at any stage. How did you play as a child? What games and adventures widened your eyes and opened your heart, made you giggle spontaneously? What experiences carry you back to that innocent time? What was just plain ol' fun? I used to enjoy tetherball; I loved my first swing at the ball and watching it fly, fly, fly high in the air, 'round and 'round that pole.

Perhaps your exhilaration lives in the pages of an old Nancy Drew mystery, or in the harmonies of a chorus you once sang in, or in hopscotch or double Dutch jump rope, or maybe in hide-and-seek. Whatever your pleasure, I encourage you to reprise it, right here in the present.

Nature gives us recreation, as well as much-needed reprieve. During the long, dark night of the 2020 shutdown, the bright spot for many of us was walking outside, a chance to catch our breath in a masked world. There's no feeling like the wind running its fingers through your hair, the morning dew settling on your cheeks, the feel of grass between your toes. Here's how Lord Byron depicted the replenishing power of the outdoors: "There is a pleasure in the pathless woods, / There is a rapture on the lonely shore, / There is society where none intrudes, / By the deep Sea, and music in its roar: / I love not Man the less, but Nature more."[5] *Rapture*—the word sums up the bliss that fresh air and solitude can bring.

Water has always been my sanctuary. My New York City apartment overlooks the Hudson River, and from my home in Key West, I can hear the ocean's riptides clapping and can smell the sea salt. It transports me to the two years my family lived in Izmir, Turkey, in an apartment smiling down over the Aegean coast. I was six when we moved there. I'd linger for hours on our back balcony, gaze at the expanse of shimmering blues and aquas, marvel at the ocean's vastness, look forward to going out fishing with my daddy. At the water's edge, I could be anyone, dream any dream and actually make it come true. And as my summer and spring have given way to autumn, the sea is still my spirit's elixir.

For you, meadows or canyons or woodlands may be the source. My friend Scarlett, the one who relocated to Arizona, has always felt restored by the desert. My prayer is that you'll move toward the landscape that makes you go "Aaaah," or whatever scene sends you into the Wonder Woman pose. That's why I think of age as a road map. On it, we rediscover the places, the memories, the people who give us life.

Joy lives outdoors, and also outside our own

insular worlds. The *message* part of the *mess* equation is the most important, because it connects us with those who share our journey. I recalled that last spring, during a week when I felt overbooked and under-rested. I realized, at the last minute, that I'd committed to attend my friend Rubem's art show on a Friday night. I thought, *Ooh, I don't feel like going... Too exhausted.* I went anyway, and the evening was splendid. I loved seeing Rubem's face light up, with so many of his tribe members in attendance, and with folks from all over admiring his work. It was beautiful. I went home thinking, *Robin, it wasn't about you.* I hadn't had to say a word. It was just about my being there for a friend. Everybody's got something... to give.

Our best times aren't behind us; they're around the next bend, and then the next. We've got to change the way we think of aging to change the way we feel about it. Let's not allow others to render us irrelevant. "No one can make you feel inferior without your consent," Eleanor Roosevelt once said.[6] Amen. Longevity is a badge of honor to be prized, not a humiliation to be hidden. We've earned every laugh line, every crease in our forehead. In each one of our wrinkles lives a story, a reminiscence, a hardship, a miracle. Own all of it. Wear it with pride, even if you choose to nip it here or tuck it there.

The world is telling us, *You've had your day. Move on.* We declare, in response, that today is our day. We're still here, still standing, hands outstretched with blessings to bestow. Let's make that the message of these glorious years: that we have endless joy to offer.

PART THREE

Stronger Than You Know

You can't control how people look at you, but you can control how far back you pull your shoulders and how high you lift your chin.

—*Elizabeth Acevedo,* With the Fire on High

Chapter 13

Vulnerability Is Strength

You are braver than you believe, and stronger than you seem, and smarter than you think.

—*Christopher Robin to Winnie-the-Pooh in* Pooh's Grand Adventure

I'll always remember what Momma told me as Hurricane Katrina ripped ashore, thundering its way toward her town in August 2005. "We're not to be fearful," she said with no quake in her voice. "Wherever we are, God is." A second later, her phone went dead. Hours after that, I was on board a plane with the *GMA* team, heading into the disaster zone. What happened next changed everything.

Mom, then in her eighties, had been too ill to evacuate. Less than a year earlier, we'd lost Daddy, our family's center of gravity and my mother's sturdy shoulder for more than fifty-five years. My sister Dorothy and her daughters, Jessica and Lauren, did not want to leave Momma, so they stayed at her home in Biloxi, just east of the Pass. The crew and I arrived in the area overnight, with a plan to report live the next morning.

When we landed and drove through the only

region I've ever called home, one with streets and neighborhoods I know by heart, I saw just how bad things were. Entire buildings had been blown to smithereens. Homes had been swept clean off their foundations. The angry currents had carried away cars, clothes, debris.

We pulled up to a barricade, and I stuck my head out the van window. The police officer recognized me—not because I was Robin Roberts from *Good Morning America*, but because I'm Lawrence and Lucimarian's youngest daughter. He'd known me and my family for decades. "Robin, glad you're here," he said. "You can go through with your crew."

My producer, Brian O'Keefe, began setting up for the live shot while I tried desperately, and failed, to reach Mom and Dorothy. "I need to go and find my momma," I said to Brian. "I cannot go on national TV without knowing my family's alive. I just can't." He nodded, I'm sure wondering if I'd make it back in time for my report. But the quiver in my voice, the water welling on my lower lids, told him I had to go.

The officer, God love that man, guided me to my mother's subdivision. Nature had lowered its steel hammer onto the township, but the damage appeared far less significant than what I'd seen coming in. We approached Mom's home, which stood tall, though there was damage to the roof. I banged on the door. "Momma?" I called out, my heart pounding in sync with every knock.

Silence.

"Who is it?" I finally heard Dorothy say.

"It's me . . . Robin," I said.

When my sister opened the door, I rushed in and scanned the living room. "Where's Momma?"

Right then, an angelic voice rang out from the back of the house, with an old gospel song I knew well. " 'What a friend we have in Jesus,' " my mother sang. " 'All our sins and griefs to bear!' "

I darted into her room. "Momma, Momma, are you okay?" I said, collapsing into her arms.

"Oh, honey, yes," she said, laughing. "I'm fine."

I told her I was there for work, but that I planned to stay with her.

"Oh, no, no, no," she said, "we'll be all right. You need to get the word out, let folks know what's going on."

I reluctantly agreed.

With the officer as my chaperone, I arrived at our live-shot location minutes before airtime. We went live at six in the morning, on Pass Road near my mom's place. I gave an account of the utter devastation, all while managing to steel myself. But when Charlie Gibson asked about my momma, boy, Niagara came pouring forth.

"Robin," he said from the anchor desk, "I know when you left here last night and flew down, you hadn't been able to make contact with your own family yet. Have you done so?"

"They're okay," I said, struggling to hold back tears.

"They're okay?" Charlie continued. "Because I know they're right there on the Gulf Coast. Mom's okay? Sisters okay?"

That opened the floodgates. "They're all right,"

I said, at last descending into sobs while thinking, *Come on, girl, pull it together.*

"All right, you take care, and give Mom our love," he said. "We'll be talking to you as the show goes on."

If you think I fell apart during the segment, you should've seen me a second later. As soon as the camera panned away, I went from mini meltdown to full-on ugly cry, weeping with all the pent-up feelings of the previous twenty-four hours.

I wept for the many who feared, as I had, that they'd never again hug their loved ones. I wept with relief that—hands raised to heaven—my family was alive. I was also crying, I must confess, because I was having a WTF moment. *What have I done?* I thought. *I just lost it on national television—with Charlie Gibson and Diane Sawyer! I'm out. Maybe I can get my job back here on the Gulf Coast, because I'm about to get the heave-ho.*

Let me remind you just how new I was as a *GMA* co-anchor then. Three months earlier, I'd stepped into this plum position, as a sports anchor turned morning show host, with much to prove. Let me also take you back to an era that now seems quaint. In 2005, serious journalists were expected to have a straight face and a stiff upper lip, to keep separate their just-the-facts reporting from their personal narratives. A Peter Jennings–like composure was the gold standard, not the heart-on-shirtsleeve approach now somewhat commonplace. This was well before TMI took hold, before reporters pulled back the curtain on their private lives via social media. And I, in my first big test, during major storm coverage, had come undone. I was sure the unraveling had ended my *GMA* career. Instead, it came to define it.

In the following days, viewers rallied around me, and even adopted my hometown. They recognized that I was speaking (more like *wailing*) from my heart. It was real. It was raw. And it allowed them to witness the kind of primal outpouring of emotion we seldom see from buttoned-up reporters, even now. Thousands had awakened that morning, unsure of whether their families and homes had been obliterated by one of the most catastrophic storms in our history. And there I stood, not just as a journalist, but as a daughter, a sister, and an aunt, someone who knew firsthand what they were feeling. My vulnerability, the very thing I thought had gotten me fired, had forged a connection between me and millions.

That is what vulnerability does: It draws us together. Counterintuitive as it may seem, scary as it may feel, when we lower our guard, we clear the way for closeness. Brené Brown, the high priestess of this principle, has shared her insight. "One of the greatest barriers to connection is the cultural importance we place on 'going it alone,'" she writes in her groundbreaking book *The Gifts of Imperfection*. "Somehow we've come to equate success with not needing anyone. Many of us are willing to extend a helping hand, but we're very reluctant to reach out for help when we need it ourselves. It's as if we've divided the world into 'those who offer help' and 'those who need help.' The truth is that we are both."[1]

Even in a culture that applauds self-reliance, our lives are interlaced, our destinies tied up as one. There's no such thing as an entirely "weak" or "strong" person. There are human beings, each perfectly imperfect, all sharing one path on this journey we call life. And along that route, we hurt. We cry. We grieve. We sometimes show our sore spots. That display, I've learned, is not an indignity. It's a superpower. It takes courage to reveal our frights and frailties.

On the day I frantically searched for Momma, I found her seated in the presence of her Maker, singing a testament to His protection. She wasn't fearless. She'd simply placed her anxieties in God's care, trusted that he'd attend to them.

She also rested in the wisdom that she and Dad embodied: We don't always have to be brave. We needn't muster fierceness ahead of every battle. What we have to be is willing: to allow others to glimpse our shaky palms, our deep uncertainties, our tremors. We must trust that, if we find ourselves short on courage, our tribe will stand in the gap. We must remember that, at our so-called weakest, we're meant to borrow strength.

Two years after Katrina leveled the Gulf Coast, that's exactly what I had to do.

❧

"We don't remember days," the poet Cesare Pavese once wrote. "We remember moments."[2] Hours pass, thousands of them over years, often without much trace. But certain instances change us. They press their thumbprints into our flesh. They write on the canvas of who we are. I'll always recall those moments, the indelible marks, that cancer left me with.

There was the instance, in summer 2007, when my doctor said the words no one's ever prepared to hear: "It's cancer." That was my ground zero, my point of no return at age forty-six. There were MRIs with a breast surgeon, the heartrending news that my cancer was triple negative—a highly aggressive form. Despair lodged in my throat as Amber cried with me. There was the moment my mom uttered the words I cling to: "Make your mess your message." Then, over months, came intense chemotherapy and radiation, each round more grueling than the last. When my hair fell out in clumps, I teared up as Mom, then in my kitchen stirring her collards, comforted me as she covered her pot. That's a moment I still laugh about. Another strong memory came when my hairstylist, Petula, shaved my head as part of a video diary we shared with *GMA* viewers—my way of turning my "mess" into awareness about the importance of early detection.

When I emerged from treatment in 2008, battered yet heartened by the groundswell of support, I thought I'd silenced cancer. Its effects roared back in 2012.

I hadn't ever heard of MDS, the mysterious blood disease that began round two of my war. When my doctor first diagnosed me with the condition, I thought he'd said MS, as in multiple sclerosis. That brief confusion was soon replaced with the real possibility that I might die soon. Not in twenty years or ten, but in one or two at most. The chemotherapy used to save my life in 2007 had now put it in peril.

I learned the severity of the disease, the dreadfully short timeline of potential breaths remaining, on the day *GMA* slid into the top spot among morning shows. I danced the limbo on that rooftop, refused to rain on my colleagues' parade, tried to focus on the fight, not the outsized fright. I choked back my sorrow, my awareness that such a celebration might be among my last.

I'd need to have a successful bone marrow transplant, doctors said, to have any real shot at beating this. Saints all over the country joined hands in prayer. My loved ones, meanwhile, also began swabbing the insides of their cheeks, hoping against hope—there's a mere three-in-ten chance that a family member will match—that a relative would become my miracle.

God heard that prayer, and Sally-Ann stepped up.

My big sister is not just one moment in my journey, but a whole slew of them strung together, kept in place by a love immeasurable. She's the reason I'm here, plain and simple. "I don't just *want* to do this, baby sister," she'd told me when we received her results. "I was born to do this." We can't put a limit on gratitude, Mom taught me, and there will never be a lid on my thanksgiving to my sister.

Our extended tribe gathered around us both in those touch-and-go days. While Sally-Ann flew to New York to prepare for the transplant, Dorothy, Butch, and the family cared for our matriarch. Mom's health had deteriorated significantly following a stroke weeks earlier, and the day before I was to begin my medical leave from *GMA*, Dorothy called to let me know that Mom had taken a turn for the worse. Sally-Ann and I immediately flew home.

Mom's speech had been impaired. She was also drifting in and out of consciousness, a state her doctors said could go on for days, weeks, months—no one could be sure. I decided to put my transplant on hold, at least for a time, as we monitored Mom's recovery. No way could I have my transplant knowing that I could lose her while I was in isolation, and thus be unable to attend her homegoing service. That wasn't an option.

That very evening after we'd rushed in from New York, and after the rest of the family had gone home, the nurse encouraged me to sit in Momma's room. "She could become lucid at any moment," she reminded me, "and you might be able to have a conversation with her." I agreed.

As Mom lay in her bed, frail yet peaceful, the nurse relayed some of the memories Mom had shared with her, encouragements meant to uplift this young woman. Even in her last days, my mother was determined to be a blessing. After recounting the many heartwarming stories my mother had detailed, the nurse ended by saying, "But you know, your momma thought she didn't do a good job with you kids."

I stared at her in disbelief. *How could that be true?*

I took Mom's hand and folded it into my mine. "Well, maybe she didn't have cookies waiting for us when we came home every day from school," I said, "But..."

And right then, as I was speaking about how wonderful my mother was, about all the sacrifices she had made for our family, she passed. I clasped her hand tightly as the tears fell. My mother had been there when I took my first breath. I was now there when she drew in her last.

My family still says that precious moment at Mom's bedside was her parting gift to me. They are right. She knew I wouldn't have that transplant while she was so ill. As she slipped out of this life and into the next, she imbued me with the strength I needed to keep going.

We celebrated Mom's legacy, the wealth of riches she bestowed during her eighty-eight years, in a homegoing service at once sorrowful and joyous. I returned to New York, heart aching, yet ready to forge ahead with my procedure less than two weeks later.

The moments from there unfolded in rapid succession, yet also in grievous slow motion. There were the ten days of high-dose chemo before the transplant itself, followed by the post-op elation that

Sally-Ann's stem cells seemed right at home in my body. There were precarious times, a whole parade of them, when we worried that infection could take out my weakened immune system. There was the low moment, late one evening in the shadows of my hospital room, when I whispered to my friend Scarlett, "Am I going to die?" She convinced me otherwise.

And through it all flowed the brightest of instances: the coworkers who came with both love and presents. (Sam, Rich, and Josh: I still wear those froggy slippers!) The colorful Prayer for Protection bracelet my friend Jo created, a reminder that my tribe stood with me. The incredible medical team that, around the clock, rushed to my aid at the slightest cough. And, of course, sweet Amber, who put her life on hold to care for me.

Then, after a full month in the protected environment of the hospital, I stepped out into fresh air, panicking about the germs I had to be inhaling. At home in quarantine, I sat for long stretches and peered out over the Hudson, heart brimming with gratitude, inching toward the critical one-hundred-day milestone I needed to reach in surviving MDS. When I crossed that line, I then fixed my gaze on another goal: becoming a thriver.

My village—not an absence of fear—got me through the most harrowing two ordeals of my lifetime. That is why I know this: Strength, the real kind, isn't about braving the behemoths on our own. It's about being willing to *receive*—to embrace the help, hope, and healing others want to give us. Vulnerability is the gateway to fortitude. An ever-deepening intimacy with those we love is the enduring treasure.

❧

"There will come a day when you won't think of cancer," a friend who's a thriver told me after I'd completed my treatment. For a long time, I couldn't imagine such a thing. When you're battling cancer, you have a game plan. You're focused on the fight, wholly consumed by it. And then, once you're released from the hospital, it's like, *Have a nice life!* And I thought, *Wait . . . but who's watching me?* Of course, I had regular checkups: first frequently (mammograms twice a year, blood work every three months), then eventually once a year, like most folks. I've sometimes struggled with long-term effects. Chemo and radiation kill the bad in your system, but also a lot of the good. I'm blessed I don't have some of the lingering results of radiation, like swelling. But my eyesight has been compromised, and I've had a bit of hearing loss; I've gotten great at reading lips.

No one really talks about the anxiety that can crop up in the years after treatment, like that little voice that whispers, *It's cancer,* every time you stub your toe or feel the slightest pain in your hip. The latter could be a symptom of age (hello, sixty!), or simply because I've been an athlete all my life. Especially if you've endured cancer twice, you find yourself looking over your shoulder, wondering if it'll return. That's where the thriver part comes in. I've surrounded myself with like-minded thrivers, those intent on flourishing, emotionally and spiritually, on this side of any major crisis. My tribe keeps my vibe on point. So does continual prayer.

This is the longest period, since 2007, that I've been healthy—ten years and counting since MDS. "Gosh, Robin, you're Benjamin Button!" a friend recently joked. "You're aging in reverse! What are you doing?"

For one thing, I'm doubling up on my water these days. Hydration is so important. I get a thrill out of keeping track of my intake, by moving a bead on my glass bottle over to the right... A small pleasure. I also keep a steady flow of vegetables in my fridge, though I still enjoy meat. Moderation is key. I'm convinced my initial cancer was caused, in part, by my heavy red-meat intake. The Roberts crew have always been carnivores. In years past, we'd all be out to dinner, placing our orders without knowing what everyone was having. Then when the waiter would present our food, we'd be looking at one another like, *What? All steak? Not a single one of us wanted the fish?* I still have an occasional burger and fries, but fresh greens have taken center stage in my plant-based diet.

I can't pinpoint the precise moment when my thriver friend's observation came true. But there did, indeed, arrive a time when cancer did not enter my consciousness. That day turned into weeks, and then into months on end. Amazing grace. I live in gratitude to the tribe that hoisted me on its back when I was flat on mine. We're stronger than we know—not because we are undaunted, but because we allow others to carry us.

Chapter 14

Beyond Your Comfort Zone

Risk: no full life occurs without it.

—Gina Greenlee

My first star turn on *Jeopardy!* was a double disaster. The year was 1999. By then, Alex Trebek, sharp-witted and impeccably dressed, had been stumping contestants for fifteen years, with clues in the form of answers. I, then an ESPN anchor, took the stage alongside two fellow sportscasters, Bob Costas of NBC Sports and Keith Olbermann, who at the time was at Fox. Each of us played for an aid organization we'd selected. And here's your clue: *The nonprofit that received a truly pitiful pittance.* You guessed it: *What is Robin Roberts's charity of choice?* That doggone buzzer was broken. That's my story, and I'm sticking to it.

Leap ahead with me to 2021, when the *Jeopardy!* team called me with another invitation, clearly having forgotten that quiz shows aren't my forte. They asked me to guest-host this time, during that monthslong stretch when they were searching for a presenter. Some of those who'd filled in clearly wanted the job for keeps, while others perhaps, like me, wondered why they were even candidates.

The November before, the world had mourned the loss of the beloved Alex, who personified grace during his battle with pancreatic cancer. I was blessed to call him a friend. One of my fondest memories is of the last time he visited the *GMA* studio. He was cracking jokes the whole time, putting the team at ease, during a period when he was fighting for his life. What a man. And what a surprise when I was asked to take the lectern he stood at for thirty-six years.

Honored as I was, I nearly declined. "No way am I doing it," I initially told Amber. "I'm terrible at game shows. Don't they remember me?"

"Well, you're not playing this time," she reminded me. "You'd be hosting."

Good point... and big difference. The invitation had come through an ABC senior executive who sounded over-the-moon excited about my appearing on behalf of *GMA*.

"I'll do it if George does it," I told him.

He laughed. "Well, George said the same thing. He's in if you're in."

Okay, then.

I did have one other reluctance. I wanted no one to think I was actually auditioning for the gig, because (a) I'm already juggling several jobs, and (b) I have zero desire to replace any of them.

Amber talked me out of that concern. "No one's going to think you want to host permanently," she said. "You're just nervous that you're going to mess up."

Exactly.

Venturing outside my comfort zone: It's a principle I love proclaiming, but sometimes find challenging to implement. Maybe you can relate. We say we want to push ourselves, and, with all of our hearts, we mean it. We make our list of audacious goals and have every intention of pursuing them. But when the time arrives to mount the diving board's ledge and plunge into unknown waters, our knees lock. Our mouths get cottony. We lose our cool. And all of a sudden, what sounded great in theory feels terrifying as we inch toward putting our ideas into practice.

Roz Savage knows what it feels like to wade into the unknown. The holder of multiple Guinness World Records, she is the first and only woman to row solo across the Atlantic, Pacific, and Indian Oceans. She's all about living a limit-free life—in her case, by braving treacherous waters. "When I was preparing for this," she writes of her Atlantic voyage, "every time someone asked me why I was doing it, I said I wanted to get out of my comfort zone. And getting outside my comfort zone is, by definition, going to be uncomfortable! Being uncomfortable doesn't mean I'm failing—it means I'm succeeding."[1]

But how do we navigate uncharted territory when apprehension arises? How do we overcome that sinking feeling that we'll make a mockery of ourselves? I'll tell you how: We march forward with a stomach that's still doing backflips. We nod yes, dust off our best diction, and book a flight out west to the *Jeopardy!* studios. It's the only way to ensure growth, not just once or twice, but over a lifetime. Fear knocks. Faith answers. Wash, rinse, repeat.

If you're looking for inspiration, it looks a whole lot like a young woman we all met in January 2021. At Biden's presidential inauguration, Amanda Gorman—rocking her gorgeous yellow suit jacket, exuding charisma to spare—riveted a country sorely in need of a bright spot. So many of us sat in rapt attention as she delivered "The Hill We Climb," a work she penned as the nation's youngest inaugural poet. (She was twenty-two at the time.)

While I was mesmerized by her rousing performance, I was most of all moved by her journey there. Amanda once struggled to pronounce the letter *R*. For a time, she avoided every word containing it. She eventually turned to poetry as a remedy. Over and over she rehearsed, until she'd mastered the sound that still doesn't naturally slide off her tongue.

She filled her inaugural poem with *R* words, half-excited and half-scared of how it would flow. And when she approached the podium on that sunny

Wednesday morning, she stepped out of her past and toward a new self.

I had a lovely conversation with Amanda the next morning on *GMA*. It's my favorite kind of interview: Catching someone right after such an event has catapulted her (or him) onto the global stage. I'm still struck by what she told me during that conversation. She said she didn't view her speech impediment as a "disability." She called it her greatest strength, one she'd worked to build upon.

All this stretching isn't for the faint of heart. It requires determination. Have I ever been tempted to turn back on the unpaved path? You bet, and not just once. I was terrified, for instance, when I transitioned from sportscasting to hard news, so much so that I briefly considered a U-turn. I'm glad I kept with it, because it led to my current position, one that has come to feel like a calling. But on my very first day at *ABC News*, I vividly remember walking through the doors—and feeling certain that everyone could hear my heart pounding.

My one day of anxiety turned into two days, then

another, and another after that. *How long will this continue?* I wondered. Then it dawned on me that I'd felt exactly the same way years earlier. During my first job, at WFPR, 14-Country, I unleashed that creek in my pants. (And by the way, my real first job was as a school bus driver, but that's another story.) I'd also been petrified in Hattiesburg, Biloxi, Nashville, Atlanta, at ESPN . . . every stop. Recalling that put me at ease.

The way I strut around *GMA* these days makes me laugh. "Careful," I can almost hear Momma saying, "you'll stumble at any moment now."

When I'm feeling short on nerve, I look to my father's example. As a student at Howard (where he met Mom), he heard about a program in Tuskegee, Alabama—a training course for Black men who wanted to become military pilots. His mother, knowing her son's dream to fly, reached out to a local New Jersey politician she'd once campaigned for. He arranged for my dad to enroll in the program. At the age of nineteen, my dad left Howard, as well as the woman he'd eventually marry. He got on a segregated train to Alabama, carrying the brown paper bags of food his mother had packed for him. She knew he'd have difficulty down south finding restaurants where a Black man would be served.

I can only imagine how fearful my young father felt, but he was steadfast in his quest to take the cockpit. Years later, he wrote a letter to my siblings and me about how God had helped him persevere. His insistence on moving beyond the comfortable led to his groundbreaking career as a pilot. His story would've ended quite differently if he'd allowed his hesitation to paralyze his will. He might never have boarded that train.

It was in my dad's memory, as well as in Alex Trebek's, that I finally agreed to host *Jeopardy!* If my dad could move through a grueling pilot's course, surely I could pronounce a few multisyllable words. My goal wasn't to mimic Alex—no one ever can—but rather to bring a little of his spirit to the taping.

I'll let you in on my friend's not-so-secret sauce: He never made the show about himself. When you look back at his nearly four decades as host, he was laser-focused on bringing out the best in the contestants, drawing out their stories during those early-game exchanges. I decided to make that my goal... to focus on the service, not on my jitters.

Speaking of service, the team at *Jeopardy!* so graciously agreed to make a donation to my charity of choice, Be The Match—an organization working to save lives through transplant. In 2012, a transplant became my lifeline, with a donation from my dear sister Sally-Ann. But a family member is a match only 30 percent of the time. The other 70 percent of the time, those in need of a transplant rely on registries like Be The Match.

We taped five shows in a single day, following a half day of rehearsals. And you know what? I thoroughly enjoyed it. The guests were delightful. (One woman, in her quest to make the show, had written fifty postcards to her local station...so this was her moment.)

"Let the light that shines within you be brighter than the one that shines on you,"[2] football coach Dabo Swinney has been credited with saying. That was my mission on the *Jeopardy!* set that day, and it's the same intention I bring to everything I do. My work is all about using an interview, a report, or even just a lighthearted comment, to uplift and inform the viewers who so kindly tune in.

And while I'm at it, I hope to constantly improve. I hope to refine my skills and up my game, to blaze past the usual and into the unfamiliar. That's what my father once did. That's what you and I have the chance to do with each new sunrise.

It's funny how worked up I was about an experience that turned out to be gratifying. In between each of the five shows, I stopped and did my Wonder Woman pose. (Yes, really.) I also took my deep breaths before and afterward.

A highlight came ahead of taping, when a writer for the show turned to me, with tears in her eyes, and said, "You're sitting in the chair where Alex sat." She then reminisced about the days, shortly before his passing, when Alex had endured enormous pain just to make it into the studio. Yet as soon as that camera light flashed red, he was ready.

She knew he and I had shared a similar health journey, and my presence somehow made her feel connected to him. That had nothing to do with me and everything to do with Alex, whose legacy of courage remains.

Chapter 15

The Best Is Yet to Come

Every breath that we take is filled with
hope for a better day.

—*Walter Mosley*

In my dressing room hangs a placard, one bearing my favorite aphorism: THIS TOO SHALL PASS... NOW WOULD BE GOOD. I chuckle every time I glance at it. It reminds me just how fleeting our lives are, how the pressure points of these years—the freneticism and the fears, the mortgages and the appointments, the to-do lists stretching into infinity—all eventually fade. We savor a pleasure. A misery replaces it. We endure a tough season. The thrill of conquest soon lifts us. Much of what we're handling seems so urgent, so make-or-break, when often, it ultimately isn't.

When I'm dealing with a situation I think is all-important, I put it through a litmus test: *In a year or two, will this matter?* Often it won't, even in a few months. That awareness changes my perspective and re-anchors me in the present. "It has been well said that our anxiety does not empty tomorrow of its sorrows," notes nineteenth-century Baptist minister Charles Spurgeon, "but only empties today of its strength."[1] How true that is.

This all sounds groovy until you're standing in a crisis, particularly a colossal one. In 2012, the doctor followed the news of my MDS diagnosis with another body blow.

"How long would I have to be away from work for a bone marrow transplant, worst-case scenario?" I asked him.

"Six months," he said with nary a stutter.

I could feel my blood pressure climbing. "Six *months*, or six *weeks*?" I said.

He repeated his original reply.

You should've seen me jump out of my chair. *This man has lost his mind if he thinks I'm not working for half a year,* I fumed. I must've put my fury on speakerphone, because that physician and his team were soon attempting to calm me.

There was no silver lining in having MDS. It was Hades, through and through. There was, however, a profound lesson, one I couldn't have known awaited.

In the stillness of quarantine—yes, a full two quarters of a year, and yet the sky somehow stayed in place—I learned how to be alone yet never lonely. I discovered how to sit with myself, without distraction, and with no urgency to reach for my phone. My explosion over the doctor's news had come and gone. *This too shall pass.*

The impact of those months of solitude has stayed, though that, too, has to be constantly renewed. Like all things on this earth, it vanishes.

It takes courage to believe the best is yet to come, and let me explain what I mean by *to come.* Our common use of certain words often doesn't capture spiritual nuance, and that's okay—you and I can translate. We understand one another when we refer to *past* and *future.* I still use both terms. But in actuality, there is no future ahead of us, nor a past in our rearview mirror. There's only what you're experiencing as you read this: one moment, one breath, followed by the next. All of life happens in the present tense, a series of "nows" marching ever onward.

So when we look ahead toward brighter horizons,

we're commemorating all things current. There's no waiting around to see how everything unfolds, no big pot of gold at the rainbow's end. There's simply choosing to take in our lives, instant by instant, with our faces raised to the sun. When we look at our journey from that perspective, it allows us to experience the full voyage: the rocky waves, the smooth sailing, the daylight, and the storm clouds. No single high tide, nor a low one, defines the trip in its entirety. That's why I work at embracing each ebb and flow.

That lesson was underscored when *GMA* finally became the number one morning show. I'm an athlete—present tense—and that means I like to win. When I was still in local television, the stations I worked at were first in their markets. It was a tremendous feeling. The same was true at ESPN: top of the ratings the whole time. *Good Morning America*, however, sat at number two, and had been there for a long while. The *Today Show* had held its superstar status for years—more than 850 weeks in total.

In 2012, every *GMA* team member—those in

front of the camera, as well as those behind it—got superfocused on chipping away at *Today*'s lead. We inched closer and closer until, lo and behold, we were right up on its tail. I'd long dreamed of the day when we'd surpass them, thought of how ecstatic I'd be.

When it happened, my then executive producer, Tom Cibrowski, literally spoke the news into my ear. I was just coming back in the studio, from what we call "the eight-thirty hellos"... that time when we converse with guests and viewers out in Times Square. Tom's gleeful voice rang out in my IFB, the earpiece anchors wear to communicate with the control room. "Because you've been here the longest," he told me, "I want you to be the first to know... We're number one."

Whoo! Major fist pump in the air. I still get chills when I recall it.

The *GMA* crew gathered upstairs with staffers from the full ABC News division. We all said a few words amid champagne toasts, celebrated our triumph as a team. This wasn't just a victory lap for the anchors, I pointed out. Every staffer who'd ever answered a phone, mailed a letter, or cut a piece of tape had a hand in it. I meant that.

Later that evening we prepared to party, though, as you know, I'd just received sobering news that I might not be here in a year. Ahead of the shindig, I and the other anchors gathered at my apartment and then walked the short distance from there to the venue. We strode down the block, giddily arm in arm, and made our way to the rooftop.

I have a framed photo of that evening, of us high-fiving and laughing and doing that limbo. Our crew knows how to cut a rug.

I remember stepping off to the side during the festivities, just briefly, to take in the scene. I thought back to all those times when I'd pined for this, when I'd said to myself, *I'm going to be the happiest I've ever been.*

Was I elated that we'd at last accomplished our goal? For sure, and I'd strive for it again. But the success didn't quite bring the nirvana I'd imagined, nor did the initial euphoria last.

That wasn't because of my diagnosis. It was, I know now, because we derive our greatest satisfaction while en route to a pinnacle, not once we surmount it. When we miss the trek—the graces and the glories and the struggles in getting there—we miss the point altogether. That's part of what it means to be brighter by the day: to be mindful of every breath we're given. Don't rob yourself of that treasure.

"We're not prisoners of our past," my dear mother often told me. "We're pioneers of an exciting future." What she was encouraging me to do was to never let my flounders, my worries, my frailties define me. We are not our histories, any more than we'll be measured by our days ahead. We are, Mom understood, architects of this moment—the only one we have for certain. We're strivers and trailblazers, powerful innovators, aligning our inventions with those of the Creator. Our finest hour isn't off in the distance. It's the one we're living, right here and now. Let's fill it with all the joy we can.

Acknowledgments

In my dressing room, I end the morning message and prayer by saying, "Have a blessed day and be a blessing." Michelle Burford has been a blessing helping me write this book. She's a talented collaborative writer, passionate about her work, as well as compassionate, guiding me to be open and share even more. I looked forward to our weekly calls chatting about faith, family, and friends.

My thanks to the Grand Central Publishing team for again being my partner in hopes of lifting up readers. My editor and friend Gretchen Young has been with me from the start with my first book, *From the Heart*. From the bottom of my heart I thank you, Gretchen.

I have such gratitude for my literary agent, Suzanne Gluck, and the entire WME family. Jon Rosen and Sharon Chang, thank you for embracing me and encouraging me to be my authentic self.

Momma said you can't put a limit on gratitude. I would need another volume to thank my amazing circle of friends and incredible coworkers. So let me close by thanking my beautiful family. Butch, Sally-Ann, and Dorothy are the greatest gifts our beloved parents ever gave me. I thank the good Lord every day that I'm your baby sista. Sweet Amber, we met on a blind date, and ever since, you've opened my eyes to true unconditional love. Being by each other's side makes every day brighter. HEEYYYY!

Notes

Introduction

1. Jian DeLeon, "Your Morning Shot: Miles Davis," GQ, September 17, 2013, https://www.gq.com/story/your-morning-shot-miles-davis-3.

Chapter 2: Make Your "One Day" Your Day One

1. Arthur Ashe, "Quotes," CMG Worldwide, licensing agent for Arthur Ashe, http://www.cmgww.com/sports/ashe/quotes/.
2. K. K. Ottesen, "Tennis Icon Billie Jean King on Fighting for Equal Pay for Women: 'Pressure Is a Privilege,'" *Washington Post*, September 3, 2019, https://www.washingtonpost.com/lifestyle/magazine/tennis-icon-billie-jean-king-on-fighting-for-equal-pay-for-women-pressure-is-a-privilege/2019/08/30/4d766498-b7b0-11e9-b3b4-2bb69e8c4e39_story.html.
3. "3 Ways Meditation Can Help Your Heart, Body, and Mind." Penn Medicine, April 3, 2020. https://www

.pennmedicine.org/updates/blogs/health-and-wellness/2020/april/3-ways-meditation-can-help-your-heart-body-and-mind. "Meditation Offers Significant Heart Benefits." Harvard Health Publishing, August 1, 2013. https://www.health.harvard.edu/heart-health/meditation-offers-significant-heart-benefits.
4. James Dillet Freeman, "The Story of the 'Prayer for Protection,'" Unity, https://www.unity.org/resources/articles/prayer-protection.

Chapter 3: Change the Way You Think to Change the Way You Feel

1. "Quotes," SuzyKassem.com, http://suzykassem.com.
2. Lori Deschene, "Tiny Wisdom: On Doubts," *Tiny Buddha*, https://tinybuddha.com/quotes/tiny-wisdom-on-doubts/.

Chapter 4: Envision Your Victory

1. Richard Bach, *The Bridge Across Forever: A Lovestory* (New York: William Morrow, 1984), 31.

Chapter 5: Give Thanks for the Glass

1. "Willie Nelson, with Turk Pipkin," *The Tao of Willie: A Guide to the Happiness in Your Heart* (New York: Gotham, 2006), xii.
2. Melody Beattie, "Gratitude," MelodyBeattie.com, December 31, 2017, https://melodybeattie.com/gratitude-2/.

3. E. Scott Geller, *Applied Psychology: Actively Caring for People* (New York: Cambridge University Press, 2016), 149. See quote in the interior of the book on Google Books at https://tinyurl.com/3w62f8xd.

Chapter 7: When Fear Knocks, Let Faith Answer

1. "Transcript: Robin Roberts ABC News Interview with President Obama," ABC News, May 9, 2012, https://abcnews.go.com/Politics/transcript-robin-roberts-abc-news-interview-president-obama/story?id=16316043.
2. Rosa Parks, with Gregory Reed, *The Faith, the Hope, and the Heart of a Woman Who Changed a Nation* (Grand Rapids, MI: Zondervan, 1994), 17.

Chapter 8: Your Tribe Determines Your Vibe

1. Dr. Tehyi Hsieh, *Chinese Epigrams Inside out, and Proverbs* (Literary Licensing, LLC, 1948).
2. Joyce Landorf Heatherley, *Balcony People* (Georgetown, TX: Balcony Publishing, 2004).
3. Oprah Winfrey, *What I Know for Sure* (New York: Flatiron Books, 2014), 196–97.
4. "Dalai Lama XIV Quotes: Quotable Quote," Goodreads, https://www.goodreads.com/quotes/7062036-when-you-talk-you-are-only-repeating-what-you-already.

Chapter 9: Get Ready for Your Suddenly

1. "Mahatma Gandhi Quotes: Quotable Quote," Goodreads, https://www.goodreads.com/quotes/806111-the-future-depends-on-what-we-do-in-the-present.

Chapter 10: Lighter by the Day

1. Martin Luther King III (@OfficialMLK3), "'Hate is too great a burden to bear,'" Twitter, May 18, 2020, 12:16 p.m.
2. Robert Enright, "Eight Keys to Forgiveness," *Greater Good Magazine*, October 15, 2015, https://greatergood.berkeley.edu/article/item/eight_keys_to_forgiveness.

Chapter 12: Make Your Mess Your Message

1. Hazel Felleman, *The Best Loved Poems of the American People* (New York: Doubleday, 1936), 537.
2. Julie Ma, "25 Famous Women on Getting Older," The Cut, *New York*, March 5, 2021, https://www.thecut.com/2021/03/25-famous-women-on-aging.html.
3. Matthew Leimkuehler and Yue Stella Yu, "Dolly Parton to State Lawmakers: Now Isn't the Time for My Statue at the Tennessee Capitol," *Tennessean*, February 18, 2021.
4. "George Bernard Shaw Quotes," BrainyQuote, https://www.brainyquote.com/quotes/george_bernard_shaw_120971.
5. George Gordon Byron, "Childe Harold's Pilgrimage," Poets.org, Academy of American Poets, https://poets.org/poem/childe-harolds-pilgrimage-there-pleasure-pathless-woods.

6. *The Yale Book of Quotations*, ed. Fred R. Shapiro (New Haven, CT: Yale University Press, 2006), 644.

Chapter 13: Vulnerability Is Strength

1. Brené Brown, *The Gifts of Imperfection: Let Go of Who You Think You're Suppose to Be and Embrace Who You Are* (Center City, MN: Hazelden, 2010), 20.
2. https://readershook.com/book/il-mestiere-di-vivere.-diario-1935-1950.

Chapter 14: Beyond Your Comfort Zone

1. Roz Savage, *Rowing the Atlantic: Lessons Learned on the Open Ocean* (New York: Simon & Schuster, 2009), 153.
2. Andrew Holleran, "Dabo Swinney Sent This Text to Tony Bennett Before the Title Game." The Spun, April 11, 2019. https://thespun.com/more/top-stories/dabo-swinney-sent-this-text-to-tony-bennett-before-the-title-game.

Chapter 15: The Best Is Yet to Come

1. *Dictionary of Quotations: From Ancient and Modern, English and Foreign Sources*, ed. James Wood (London: Frederick Warne, 1893), 198, https://www.gutenberg.org/cache/epub/48105/pg48105-images.html.

About the Authors

Robin Roberts is co-anchor of ABC's *Good Morning America*, and the *New York Times* bestselling author of the memoir *Everybody's Got Something.* Under her leadership, the broadcast has won six Emmy Awards for Outstanding Morning Program and has been ranked as the number one morning show in America for nine consecutive seasons. She also serves as the president at Rock'n Robin Productions, where she actively oversees creative content and new business partnerships. Previously, Roberts was a contributor to ESPN. In addition to the Emmys, she has been the recipient of numerous other awards, including a Peabody, for her documentation of her own medical odyssey, and the Arthur Ashe Courage Award. A native of the Mississippi Gulf Coast, she now resides in New York City.

Michelle Burford served as Robin Roberts's collaborative writer. She is a number one *New York Times* bestselling author who has partnered on twelve books, with legends including Cicely Tyson, Alicia Keys, Halle Berry, and Simone Biles. She is also a founding editor of *O, The Oprah Magazine* and a former *Essence* magazine editor. A native of Phoenix, she lives in New York City. Visit MichelleBurford.com.